*Judy + John —
Thank you for sharing
the journey*

[signature]

MEETING THE MANTIS

SEARCHING FOR A MAN IN THE DESERT
AND FINDING THE KALAHARI BUSHMEN

John Ashford

D1738314

A PEACE CORPS WRITERS BOOK

MEETING THE MANTIS: SEARCHING FOR A MAN IN THE DESERT
AND FINDING THE KALAHARI BUSHMEN
A Peace Corps Writers Book
An imprint of Peace Corps Worldwide

For more information, contact peacecorpsworldwide@gmail.com.
Peace Corps Writers and the Peace Corps Writers colophon are trademarks of
PeaceCorpsWorldwide.org.

The cover design by Zach Hooker.
The Bushmen and Tsodilo Hills pen and ink drawings on the cover are by Michelle Poston.
The mantis chapter graphics are based on an original painting by Genevieve Ashford.
Text design and layout by Marian Haley Beil.

Some names and identifying details have been changed to protect the privacy of
individuals.

ISBN-13: 978-1-935925-60-6
Library of Congress Control Number: 2015947825

First Peace Corps Writers Edition, October, 2015

The Colors in the Rainbow

The Rainbow is yellow in that part which lies above; the piece which seems red lies below. For the Mantis, who is also yellow, lies above, and Kwammang-a lies below. For the Mantis is the one whose part above is yellow, and that part which lies below is red, while that part which is above is yellow.

It is the Rainbow. Men call it Kwammang-a. Therefore we who are children say "Kwammang-a" to it, because the grown-up people said Kwammang-a to it. Therefore we say Kwammang-a to it. Then people say: "The Rainbow stands yonder and the rain will break."

— Bushman story from *The Mantis and His Friends*
by Dorothea Bleek;
the stories were collected by her father, W. H. I. Bleek, in the 1870s

BOTSWANA

MILAGE
Tonota – Tsodilo Hills – Tonota /1240 mi
Tonota – Gaborone /252 mi
Tonota – Dkar – Ghanzi – Okwa Valley – Gaborone /1466 mi

Table of Contents

Prologue

My wife Gen and I were in our mid-fifties when we went to Botswana in 1990 as Peace Corps Volunteers to work as teachers. At home in Seattle, I had worked in education for thirty years, but I'd reached a point of burnout. I was restless for new experiences.

I had always wanted to join the Peace Corps. The wish arose from my idealism in the early 1960s as well as my desire for adventure — but it was also partly stimulated by an anthropology class I'd taken in college.

For that class I read Laurens van der Post's *Lost World of the Kalahari* (1958) about the Kalahari Bushmen who lived in a village in the Tsodilo Hills in Bechuanaland — now Botswana. The Bushmen, who are the indigenous people, or First People, of southern Africa, are also known as the San. Van der Post reported that the San valued group harmony. Men and women worked as equals in decision-making, and after a hunt, food was shared with the entire community. The men were prophets and healers, and the women possessed special powers and ESP and knew if there would be game for dinner long before a hunting party returned.

Another book that shaped my fond attitude about the Bushmen was *The Harmless People* (1959) by Elizabeth Marshall Thomas. She described them as shy, non-competitive people, and their folktales were full of heroes who won victories through cleverness rather than confrontation.

My college friends and I had many conversations about less materialistic life styles and the San seemed to be proof that such an idea was possible.

Three rugged stone hills at Tsodilo rise out of the desert to a height of nearly 1,000 feet, and according to van der Post, in San folklore the hills were living entities. The tallest was called Male Hill and nearby, massive but not as tall, was Female Hill. In San mythology, the third hill was sometimes a child and, in other stories, another female and a temptation to frequently straying Male Hill. In those stories, though he might be unfaithful, Male Hill had to return because the only source of water flowed from Female Hill.

The Tsodilo Hills contain more than 4,500 rock art paintings, some dating back 2,000 years, and have been designated an UNESCO World Heritage Site. In his book *Believing and Seeing* (1981), David Lewis-Williams quotes several scholars who agree that there is a religious reason for the subjects of the rock art. It is a sacred site. The animals depicted are sacred to the San, and this is especially true of the eland. Lewis-Williams quotes Patricia Vinnicombe who wrote in *People of the Eland*, who wrote, "As the wind was one with man, so man was one with the eland."

In the late 1980s I began to think seriously of quitting my job and joining the Peace Corps, but Gen required some convincing. She also had a career, and we both had grown children from previous marriages. Neither of us had ever worked overseas, so in 1990, I quit my job and we went to Thailand to find work that would accommodate the two of us. During that summer we worked in a refugee camp south of Bangkok.

After our stint in Thailand, we returned briefly to Seattle, where we found out that we had been accepted into the Peace Corps and assigned to Botswana.

At the time, we were house-sitting, and in one of the homes where we stayed I found a magazine article describing the ritual trance dance of the Kalahari Bushmen. It triggered memories of books I'd read years earlier about the San, and for the first time it began to sink in that the Kalahari Desert was in Botswana. Our assignment began to feel as if something in my life had come full circle.

The possibility of contact with the Bushmen and the wealth of rock art in the Tsodilo Hills tugged at me as soon as we arrived in Botswana.

Meeting the Mantis

Searching for a man in the desert and finding the Kalahari Bushmen

1 Losing Our Way in the Kalahari

On a bright, sunny day in Botswana, we made camp in a beautiful spot on the banks of the Okavango River. It felt like paradise on earth. Just a few yards from our tents the river curled and foamed under the lip of the bank. Several pairs of gray parrots called from the trees overhead and we heard the bark of baboons in the distance.

Gen and I hadn't been in Africa long and this was our first trip into the Kalahari Desert. It was our spring vacation from teaching and a few months after we had completed our Peace Corps training, and we were on our way to visit the San village in the Tsodilo Hills.

The drive to the Hills from our home in Tonota — across Botswana — was comparable to a trip across Texas. Because of the distance, the unpaved and poorly maintained roads, and our limited schedule, we would have only one day — tomorrow — for our visit in the village.

We were joined by two other teachers, Jim, who was British, and Marjorie, a Volunteer like us. All of us were novice travelers. We shared costs and traveled together in the cab of a small Toyota truck.

Following our arrival that afternoon we had made camp near a resort. In the evening, the four of us took a sunset cruise on the river, ate a sumptuous meal, and topped it all off with brandy. Returning to camp, everybody had a pleasant glow.

For the past several days Marjorie and Jim had been quarreling — and Gen and I were too often stuck in the middle of it — but that evening I noticed Jim and Marjorie crawl into the same tent. I hoped that the pleasant night had healed the rift.

The next morning I arose at sunrise and found a hippo wandering through our camp. I watched him until he ambled back into the river, then roused our friends so we could get an early start. After tea and a quick breakfast, we left camp knowing we could look forward to returning that evening to this garden of tall lush trees, wildlife, and colorful singing birds.

We drove until the road forked. There I got out of the cab and twisted the hubs of the front wheels to put the truck into four-wheel drive, because we were heading west along a narrow track of deep sand into an arid forest of stunted brown trees. The truck rocked slowly through potholes and ruts. Every mile or so our tires bogged down in the sand and we'd have to dig a wheel free. The metal of the truck was searing hot, and as we shoveled we had to be careful not to touch it. Inside the truck the heat was intense.

In the hope of generating a breeze, the windows were open, but along with the breeze came a swarm of small black flies. Gen, beside me, blew air through her lips.

"Phew," she said. "They keep getting in my mouth."

In the backseat, Marjorie beat the air vigorously with her hat to keep the insects away from her face. We were learning why the Kalahari was sometimes called "the land filled with flies."

Despite the discomfort, I was high with anticipation. We were on our way to meet a San group and see their rock art! The village was also an important place historically. Archeologists have found evidence that the village in the Tsodilo Hills has been in continuous use for at least 20,000 years, a time when the waters of a lake lapped against a nearby shore. In my mind, the San had lived there forever.

The truck's motion became hypnotic. The dry landscape made it easy for me to lose myself in my imagination. I imagined San hunters tracking antelope and small game. Under a wall of brush looming ahead, I half expected to see the naked legs of a hunter and his down-pointed bow, waiting for the movement of a desert hare. When the daydream receded, I saw only the tan burnt leaves of desert scrub, and although it was still morning, the sun was almost directly overhead.

As I drove, I remembered photographs and films I'd seen of San gatherers, women in skin aprons and shoulder bags, poking in the sandy earth with digging sticks, probing for tubers and edible roots. Those were the pictures in my naive mind, images of nomadic hunter-gatherers following a way of life as old as humankind. People in a land where resources were scarce who fostered habits of harmony and cooperation. I recalled seeing a film years earlier about Bushman hunters who killed a giraffe and then shared the meat among the entire band.

After two and a half hours, Jim asked from the backseat, "What're we looking for . . . I mean landmarks and such?"

"Limestone peaks?" Gen answered without much conviction. "Sticking up out of the desert?" The truth was, we weren't really sure, but none of us wanted to drive past and miss the goal of the entire trip.

The road narrowed even further and the truck continued its rocking, swaying motion. Occasionally the side mirrors knocked against thin trunks of scrub trees.

Four hours after leaving camp, the road circled the base of a large rock outcropping and we suddenly saw huts. We had arrived.

I stopped the truck when we came to a circular rail fence that enclosed a group of huts facing inward, some made of mud, and others of grass. Several large trees shaded the area. A dozen men and women, small in stature and olive-skinned, were clustered near the fence staring silently at our truck.

Three men walked toward us, hesitated and then began a conversation among themselves. They spoke in quiet tones, full of rustling sounds and clicks. They were Dzu Twasi, formerly known as the Kung and one of the many San groups in Botswana.

The San are considered by some anthropologists to be one of the most ancient populations in the world. Their language of clicks is very likely derived from the earliest forms of spoken language — the Mother Tongue. I knew about their language of clicks, but I'd never heard it spoken. I could not recognize any of their words, but as I listened it felt as though I was hearing the echoes of time. Hearing it spoken was like listening to a hunter step carefully over twigs or hearing the wind sweep across a field of grass.

Finally, one of the three moved toward me, gesturing as though to tell me something. He was barefoot and wore just a pair of khaki shorts with an animal skin in his a belt loop. He looked like the Bushmen I had seen in photographs. He spoke and gestured with his arms, but I didn't understand what he was trying to tell me.

Then I heard a voice say in English, "See headman."

For the first time I noticed a lean-to in the shadows about ten feet away. Inside two youths lay back braced on their elbows with their feet crossed. Then one of the young men sat up, leaned forward, pointed down the road, and called out, "Headman one kilometer. They saying you." After speaking, he returned to the universal posture of a teenage male. The only thing missing from the picture was a TV set.

I called to the men in my best Setswana, "We'll be back shortly." The man with the animal skin belt raised his hand to wave, acknowledging that he understood. I got back in the truck and started the engine.

Gen asked, "Where are we going?"

"To see the headman, I guess. Other than that, haven't a clue," I answered. "Down the road. We'll find out together."

We drove down the road about ten minutes until we reached a mud hut surrounded by corn stalks. Outside the hut sat a large man on a carved wooden stool. He had a corncob pipe sticking out from between his teeth. Definitely not a Bushman, his skin was a deep brown, almost black. He was solidly built with a broad chest. I guessed that he was a Humbukush tribesman.

I got out of the truck and extended my hand. Intuitively, I understood we had to pay this man although I was not clear about the reason. The arrangement seemed vaguely feudal. The large man rose from his stool and greeted me with a handshake. Of course, he knew what we had come for and looked happy to see us.

I greeted him in Setswana. "*Dumela.*"

"*Ehe, wa dzu.*"

"We want to see the rock art. The people sent us here." I jerked my thumb in the direction of the village.

He started to say something, but was interrupted by a coughing fit. Deep and rasping, the cough shook his body in a violent spasm.

"Ten *pula*," he said when he recovered. He smiled, but his eyes were dull and ringed with red. It was clear that he was ill.

"Do I pay you?"

"Ehe." Yes.

I pulled two fives from my pocket.

He accepted the money, and then stuffing it in his pocket, asked, "Aspirin? You have?" He patted the side of his head. "Very hurt. Bad today."

Inside the truck, several pairs of hands rustled through traveling bags. A bottle of Tylenol passed through the open window.

"It's all I have," said Gen.

I shook out half a dozen tablets into the pink flesh of the man's outstretched hand, and then, after checking in the bottle to see how many were left, shook out a few more.

When we returned to the village, the three men were squatting in the shade of a large mongongo tree near the entrance to the compound. We all climbed out of the truck and stood there while half a dozen women waved trinkets for sale — bracelets and necklaces made from ostrich shell beads. Whenever one of the three men tried to say something to our group, the women shouted, drowning out the men's voices.

The man with the animal skin belt introduced himself as M'pao. He gestured toward the man next to him who wore a green sweatshirt. This man would be our guide. Then M'pao opened his hands in front of his chest, spreading ten fingers, making the gesture twice.

From the lean-to, the teenager who translated earlier called out, "Pay twenty!"

I peeled twenty pula from a ball of paper money in my pocket. The bill felt soggy with sweat. As soon as the women saw the money, they all screamed. When I handed the bill to the man in the sweatshirt, they screamed louder. They raised their arms, waved necklaces, and shook bracelets in the air. The screaming was not directed at me, however.

One woman, who was wearing a white blouse, red wrap skirt, and a blue cloth tied on her head, walked over to M'pao and began speaking angrily close to his face as she braced her knotted fists on her formidable hips. As her fists — still holding ostrich bead trinkets — pressed hard into the fabric of her skirt, the trinkets dangled at her side. There was a recognizable familiarity between the woman and M'pao that made me think they were married.

I gathered from her tone that she was upset about the distribution of wealth and that she spoke on behalf of the others as well. She finally backed off and rejoined her group. Watching this dissension, I asked myself, *Am I in the right place? Isn't this the culture that shares everything? That values harmony and balance between its members?*

These people were not fulfilling my long-held romantic notions instilled long ago in an anthropology class and reinforced by many books. What I was witnessing went against the grain of everything I'd ever learned about this culture.

Our guide, the man in the green sweatshirt, was named Selook. M'pao introduced us and I extended my hand eagerly. Selook's hand was limp. The top of his head reached the middle of my chest. I guessed he was about four feet eight inches in height. In addition to his sweatshirt, he wore shorts and a crumpled, tan golf hat. Selook might have been a suburban man ready to mow the lawn, except there was no lawn. His hat, with the rim pressed low on his brow, cast a dark shadow across his eyes and gave his deeply lined face an unhappy expression.

Without a gesture or a wave, Selook walked off toward a rock face. He led us up a trail through gray sand. His eyes were focused downward, his head hung down, and his hands were thrust into the pockets of his shorts. He looked like a man embarking on a grim task.

For a few minutes we followed a trail under a shelf of overhanging rock. Selook led us around the base of Female Hill, which is where much of the rock art is. He took us to view the well-known glyphs and pictographs of the Tsodilo Hills — described as the Louvre of Bushman art by Laurens van der Post and reproduced in books by him and other writers who have lived and worked with the Bushmen. Some of the rock art we were viewing could be thousands of years old. No one seemed to know for sure. All of the art I'd read about for so long was there: the lion with huge shoulders and mane and the eland antelope, with its chest swelling into a muscular triangle. There were trickster and shamanic images. There were many images of the hunt — Bushmen hunters with penises erect, showering arrows on a herd of unmoving antelope. All of the images represented some kind of power. In a shadowy rock niche, there were mysterious glyphs — oval shapes containing grids with dots and cross-hatchings. Questions about their meaning have kept scholars busy for years.

Selook guided us around the hillside to view the images on the rock, every image an icon, the hillside a temple. We followed Selook through this religious spot for two hours or so and forgot about the tensions among the people in the village. Instead, there was something almost narcissistic about the way we were caught up in our individual struggles for a better photograph.

At one point we walked a trail that wound past a boulder the size of a house and alongside a sloping rock wall. Walking under a stone overhang, we climbed the trail to a crack in the limestone. Then, rounding the base of the hill, we entered a grove of thorn trees where we marched in dappled light. A small Francolin hen — its face bright red and its plumage blending perfectly with the dry knee-high grass — scurried into bushes ahead of us. Remembering pictures of Bushman techniques for snaring ground birds, I tried to engage Selook in a sign language conversation. Gesturing, I acted out the snare, the bird walking into it, and the capture. I smiled as I made the signs.

A glint of sunlight on his hat made his expression look darker. His hands were still jammed into his pockets. A pained expression crossed his face as he stood politely, watching my gyrations. He let me finish and nodded to show he understood. Then his eyes shifted abruptly and Selook returned to the task at hand guiding us toward more indentations decorated by ancient hunters and walls scarred by the smoke of old campfires where a shaman may have led a trance dance.

As I followed behind him, I realized that this was his way of changing the subject. I suppose his clouded expression could be translated as, *Spare me! I have had enough of amateur anthropologists and would-be white Bushmen.*

Eventually the path circled back to the village where M'pao waited. He was squatting in the shade talking with another man who was wearing rumpled trousers and a dirty T-shirt. The other was standing awkwardly, as if he had been injured. His face was gray as dust. The puffiness around his eyes suggested a serious hangover. A few feet away, six women hunched down, feet flat on the sand, knees in the air. Everyone ignored us. It was a relief. There were low conversations in the clicking, rustling speech. A grandmother with a weathered face, the gold skin of her bare arms deeply seamed, chatted with a small child. Two younger women held souvenir strings of beads and laughed, sharing a joke. Everyone's tone of voice was subdued.

Quiet.

That was what I expected when we had first arrived hours earlier.

I wondered for a moment if the group was returning to a more traditional mode of behavior, but that thought was soon dispelled. At some signal of which I was not aware, the group made a decision to acknowledge our return and abruptly their behavior changed. The two women who had been chatting amiably suddenly began waving strings of white ostrich shell beads in our direction, each crowding the other for our attention.

Gen walked over to where the women displayed the jewelry, holding necklaces in their hands. She inspected several bracelets, letting the rough textured shells and seeds run through her fingers. Marjorie then aimed her camera at the group, but a woman shouted, indicating that Marjorie would have to pay if she wanted to take a photo. Marjorie let her camera dangle from a strap around her neck while she fished a five pula bill out of a small purse and gave it to the woman. Then another woman protested, Marjorie pulled out a five pula note for her. She aimed again and snapped her picture.

M'pao approached me.

"Show?" he said, holding up the palm of his hand toward me, as though he were a traffic policeman stopping traffic. I waited while he walked to a hut at the far edge of the circle. Then M'pao returned carrying a Bushman hunting kit with a three-foot bow and a quiver of arrows.

He held it up and pointed at his chest.

"You made it?" I asked. He nodded. "How much?" He gave me the same gesture he had made earlier when we arranged our guided tour.

"Twenty?" I asked.

The young men in the lean-to translated, we sealed the transaction, and M'pao gave me permission to take a photo. When the woman in the red skirt saw the money changing hands, she began shouting at M'pao again.

M'pao ignored her and slung the hunting kit over his shoulder. I focused my camera. Through the lens I watched M'pao puff up his chest and pull his stomach muscles tight. In the viewfinder he had the proud bearing of a hunter, while a few feet away the woman I assumed to be his wife shouted at him. His dignity seemed impervious to her attacks and M'pao remained perfectly photogenic. The woman disappeared into a hut before I finished taking my picture.

My attitudes had been shaken by the time we drove away from Tsodilo. Friction between the genders was obvious, but puzzling. I had always understood that decisions among the San people were made by consensus, and that the people shared among themselves. If so, why would the woman be so offended when Selook was chosen to lead a tour or that M'pao sold me a bow and arrow kit? I could understand if the wealth was being distributed unfairly — she was standing up for herself. But at the same time her anger seemed over the top. They seemed to be a group of people in crisis.

I wondered what had happened. Had an adviser come here and told these people that everything about their way of life was wrong? I could imagine a development worker or a consultant on tourism lecturing them: *It's a tough world out there. Forget about cooperation and sharing. For you to progress you have to learn to compete.*

There was something else I couldn't understand. Why did I have to pay the headman, a Humbukush tribesman? He was not San? It was an indication that the San were not regarded very highly — it was a feudal arrangement.

In the waning shadows of the day, we made our way to the main road. Back on this somewhat better maintained surface, the truck picked up speed. When I looked into the side view mirror I saw fine gray sand rolling off the tires and making a coil in the air behind, like a thread unraveling from a tightly wound spool.

2 A Flip Remark

As we drove away from the campsite near Tsodilo the next morning, there were plenty of reminders that we had left paradise — or perhaps that paradise had been lost.

My anticipation and excitement of the previous day had turned to doubt and disillusion. In addition, the tensions in the back seat of the truck returned almost immediately. Jim and Marjorie had begun snarling at each other — and we had three-days ahead of us. The trip home would be trying for all of us.

Jim and Marjorie had been dating before we left on our trip, but they lived in villages separated by miles of bad roads, dry hills, and brown savannah — which is to say, they seldom saw each other. Apparently most of their time together before this trip had been spent in a state that lent itself to overlooking annoying behavior. If they needed a cure for their affection, they'd found it sitting next to each other in a jouncing truck for ten days.

Marjorie was an artist, and she was attracted to beautiful things, gorgeous creatures, and new experiences. Because she never wanted to close the door on a new experience, it was difficult for her to make a plan. She felt that a vacation should be as open-ended as possible and should allow her time to take as many photographs as she wanted.

Jim was a math teacher with a strong need for order and predictability. In our conversations about our travel plans, the topics of thrift and efficiency were high on his list.

Jim had a ritual when we stopped to take a break. He would open his box of English Dunhills, light up a cigarette, lean against the back bumper, and stare into the desert. At the agreed departure time, Jim snuffed out his cigarette. But Marjorie always wanted one last photograph of a flower she had found, a bird she was stalking, or some newly discovered desert plant. Invariably, Jim was put out by the inefficiency her actions caused — a departure delayed, a cigarette not enjoyed to the fullest, someone not following the rules. He waited by the door of the truck impatiently, sighing loudly.

The day after our visit to Tsodilo, the first day of our trip home through the Okavango Delta, we drove over terrible roads for hours on our way to find a campsite, and then conflict arose the moment we got out of the truck.

"There's a lovely spot," Marjorie said. "Right over there." She pointed to a spot about fifty yards from the truck where a pair of tall arching sausage trees grew, their branches heavy with hanging fruit and their mossy trunks bent under the weight. Late afternoon sunlight slanted through the trees bathing the area with a soft greenish light.

"I wouldn't camp there if you paid me," Jim barked. "Look, there are baboons in those trees."

He was right. We all saw them. The entire troop sat in the thick branches, picking lice and staring at us with suspicion. Their young jumped up and down on the swaying branches, playing a chasing game.

"Besides, that spot is too near the reeds. That means mosquitoes." He pointed out another place, closer to where we were parked. "On the other hand, if we make camp here, we have a fire pit for cooking, level places for our tents, and a source of firewood."

Marjorie made a noise of disgust.

"Did we drive all this way just to camp in a boring patch of dirt?" She was usually soft spoken. I'd never heard her speak angrily before. "Why did we come here? The beauty of the place is in the plants and trees, wildlife, greenery. And you want us to camp in a parking lot?"

Her tone of voice implied more. She left a string of choice insults unsaid.

Gen and I were reluctant to intervene. For one, I didn't have the energy. I had been driving for hours and my needs were simple: I wanted a place to cook, eat, and stretch out. But we were at an impasse and finally my fatigue won out and I made a suggestion, "Why don't we flip a coin? Heads or tails?"

My suggestion was answered with blank stares, but I pulled a coin from my pocket. The silver coin was Botswana's equivalent of an American quarter, but there were no heads or tails; instead, it had a shield on one side and a lion on the other. Between my thumb and index finger, I held the coin for all to see. "Okay, how about shields and lions?"

They walked away before I had a chance to toss the coin. Jim and Marjorie both seemed to think I was trivializing their conflict so I succeeded in bringing them together in one way: they were united in not speaking to me, but they weren't speaking to each other either. In fact, no one spoke for a long time. We spent a very silent evening.

On the second day of our trip through the Kalahari, we returned to the paved road. It was nearly sunset when I turned the truck off the highway and into a lodge near a village called Nata. The lodge was in a beautiful oasis in the middle of an arid land. A row of tall ilalla palm trees marked the entrance. I nosed the truck into a parking space.

Gen and I found a spot to sleep under an ilalla palm in the lodge campground just behind a row of luxury chalets. I unpacked the tent and ground cloth from the truck and then we did a shuffle across the sand before setting it up. Our dance had the double purpose of leveling a space in the Kalahari sand and clearing the area of any scorpions that might be lurking. I had no idea where Marjorie and Jim were. They had taken to making camp as far apart from each other — and us — as possible.

It was after dark when Gen and I finally climbed into our tent.

Lying inside I noticed that every star was visible through the tent's mesh walls. A generator hummed in the background, but I paid no attention to it. I was happy to just relax. Kuu-ku-ku. Kuu-ku-ku. Mourning doves cooed in the trees surrounding the campground; this was the ubiquitous sound of Africa.

Gen fell asleep immediately. I listened to her rhythmic breathing as I watched the Southern Cross and an unknown constellation rising in the south. That constellation circled the Southern Cross all night. The name of the constellation remained a mystery to me, but I'd seen it often and it always reminded me of a huge scorpion in the sky, its tail forward in an aggressive posture.

As I puzzled over the name for the stars making up the distinct grouping, I became aware of the glow from the rising moon and began nodding off to sleep. At that moment the sound of rattles, hand clapping, and a man's voice calling out pulled me back to wakefulness. Several other voices joined in and began to sing. The shaking of the rattles became more insistent. The music makers were close enough that I could hear the shuffling sound of their feet on hard-packed sand. A party, I thought. I was used to hearing celebrations with lots of singing and drumming in my own village and I always hoped they'd end at a reasonable hour.

But this music seemed different from what I heard in my village — a bit more chaotic, for one thing. Voices chimed in without consideration for other parts, harmonies were more dissonant. The singing went on and on until I became aware that it was a chant. The sharp rhythm of rattles continued without a break as the full moon rose higher in the sky. Its brilliance made the inside of the tent seem bright as day.

At eleven-thirty the generator motor from the lodge shut down. The hum had become a drone that I was hardly aware of until it stopped. Electric lights around the lodge went dark. The moon cast ragged shadows of palm fronds overhead.

The chanting continued. Despite that, I must have drifted off. At some point, I awoke and listened. One man's voice rang out as a high-pitched strained cry. Other voices lagged in their response as if the singers were tiring.

Throughout the night, half-awake and barely aware, I sensed the movement of the moon, the rotating path of stars around the Southern Cross, the shadow of palms moving across the tent. I heard the chanting, rattles, slapping of feet, the volume rising and falling. Throughout the rest of the night, I drifted between sleep and consciousness.

Toward morning the rattles still shook and feet beat the ground, but something had changed. Earlier, the beat slowed or quickened as the singers' energies ebbed and flowed. Now the beat was steady, the chanting was strong, and the rattles buzzed. More surprising to me, the mourning doves seemed to join the singers as they responded to the leader's voice calling out. Kuu-ku-ku. Kuu-ku-ku. The presence of the doves woke me up to one fact: This wasn't a party. What was I listening to? Was it a trance dance ceremony — a ritual of healing used by the Kalahari Bushmen?

The eastern sky glowed and I heard the birds moving somewhere in the branches of the trees. At the break of dawn the chanters, dancers, and rattle shakers stopped. The air was still. Then the doves' kuu-ku-ku, kuu-ku-ku interrupted the silence once more.

In the morning Gen and I strolled over to the lodge's outdoor restaurant and picked out a table. The air was cool. We each poured ourselves a cup of coffee from a heated urn. Gen was carrying her sketch pad and had it open on the table before either of us had taken our first sip.

I sat still for a few minutes staring into empty space. In my mind I still heard the rhythmic throb of the dance that had gone on all night. Sounds of shaking rattles and the shuffling of feet. I didn't know what to think about what I'd heard. The sounds had left me in a daze.

On the way to the restaurant I had loaded our tent into the truck and overheard Jim muttering to himself, "What the hell did she do with my knapsack?" I saw he was having trouble finding his cigarettes, but I said nothing and continued on my way.

A few minutes later Jim appeared in the restaurant with his box of Dunhills in hand. He helped himself to coffee from the urn and joined us in the center of the small courtyard under the morula tree. Nearby, brilliantly colored birds dabbled at a tray of birdseed and fruit scattered there by restaurant staff. Gen's gaze was fixed on the birds. The scratch of her pen on a page in her sketch pad was audible as the three of us sat quietly letting the steam from our cups drift upward.

The echo of noises in my head continued from the night before — the call and response chanting and the voices chiming in with dissonant harmonies. In our village, when the singers finished a song there was a musical signal — *Okay, boys, we've sung that song, let's do another.* But the chanting and rhythm I heard during the night had continued without a break. I remembered the mourning doves as they entered the chant, their kuu-ku-ku answering in perfect time. The thought persisted that I'd been listening to the sounds of a healing ritual.

The scratch of Gen's pen on paper brought me back to the present. I watched as she filled in her drawing of the birds feeding at the tray of fruit. I couldn't believe I'd heard a trance dance happening just a hundred feet from where we camped.

Across the patio I spotted Marjorie walking under the branches of a camel thorn tree. She glanced from one table to another, apparently considering her options. It was clear she didn't want to sit at the same table with Jim. The last few days had the feel of a forced march with the two of them side by side in the backseat. Sarcastic remarks had flown like darts through the vehicle. I wouldn't have objected if she'd made another choice, but Marjorie must have decided that sitting at our table would be the polite choice. She resolutely stepped over to the heated urns at the buffet table, poured herself a cup of tea, and joined our group.

The silence of the moment was broken by the scraping of her vinyl chair on concrete as she sat down.

I asked, "Did the chanting keep anyone awake last night?"

"Not me," Gen said.

Jim chimed in, "Slept like a log."

After a slight pause Marjorie said with forced cheer, "I had the funniest dream last night."

Jim took a final pull on his cigarette and, stubbing it into an ashtray, gave a wry laugh. "I'm happy I don't remember dreams. People always tell me the silliest things about their dreams."

Marjorie ignored him. "I dreamed baboons came into my tent. Really! They were jumping on my tent poles." Her tone of voice suggested there might be more.

"Never dream, myself." Jim pulled his box of cigarettes from his shirt pocket, took out another, and lit up. Tipping his head back, he exhaled into the cool air.

"They were doing acrobatics," Marjorie said.

"I dreamed, too," said Gen. "I dreamed I walked up a sandy hill, a dune, and all of a sudden found myself between two enemy armies. One minute I was walking through the sand, minding my own business, the next I was ducking bullets these armies were shooting at each other."

Gen's voice had a kind of exaggerated sincerity. I couldn't be sure — was she making this up? Was this really a dream?

"It was such an unusual dream for me," she continued. "I never dream about warfare. But there I was in the middle. I don't even know who was fighting. Maybe it was Germany and Russia. They were shooting. I was ducking. Not that I was really afraid. It was kind of exciting. I popped my head up, then ducked."

I sipped the last drop from my cup and considered a refill.

"Zing zing zing," Gen said. "Bullets bouncing everywhere."

After breakfast we had a short drive along a paved road before dropping off first Jim and then later Marjorie at their houses. Gen and I then continued on, back to the college. We'd be home by dinnertime.

Driving away from Nata Lodge, the chant was still reverberating in my head. I began to make an association from my childhood with what I'd heard during the night. My childhood coincided with World War II and it was a time when both my parents worked in defense industries.

My father, with a master's degree in music, was hired as a pipe-fitter in a shipyard. He later became a welder. My mother, who had nurtured a desire to be a poet, worked at the Boeing Aircraft Company — doing the same job as Rosie the Riveter.

It wasn't unusual for me to be left on my own. For me, it was just the way we lived. Even so, as a child I never got used to being alone in an empty house. I did anything I could to be away from the house at times when my parents were gone.

Many Saturdays I walked aimlessly to a business district about a mile away. I read the marquees on movie theaters that I passed. I smelled the fragrance emanating from a commercial bakery. Then I would amble back through a park at the top of the hill, sometimes visiting the art museum, and return home through an old cemetery.

After school, I did my best to get invited to a friend's place. Still, there were days when I came home from school to an empty house. I tried to find things to read or projects to work on. But the creaking and groaning and cracking of the old house always made me think someone or something was walking stealthily across the floor of one of the upstairs bedrooms. At times, I felt an unexplainable breeze, as if an intruder had just opened a door or window. In those moments, the only thing I knew to do was find some kind of exotic music to play from my father's collection of 78 rpm records.

My father loved jazz and had a large collection of early recordings, but he also took an interest in a new field, later known as ethnomusicology. He was particularly interested in the relationship of jazz to its African and Caribbean origins. As a child, I tagged along once when he attended a lecture by a scholar who had made recordings of music in the field. After that lecture, my father acquired albums of rituals performed in remote tribal locations.

These became my favorite records to play. I turned up the volume as loud as I could and hopped around the living room in rhythm to the drums.

The leader of the chanting called out, *"Jay-ke-ke ke-ke-Jah."* The chants were exciting. The drumming stirring. Along with the other tribal dancers, I responded, *"Jay-ke-ke ke-ke-Jah."*

The language was unintelligible, but the music filled the rooms and the chant seemed appropriate in my effort to control the spirits of fear and loneliness that occupied the shadowy voids in the house.

3 A Stroke of Luck

After we returned from the Tsodilo Hills school began and I became engrossed in my teaching duties.

A year passed and Gen and I both had begun to assimilate the fact that our Peace Corps service would be ending in about eight months. The anticipation made me feel a certain amount of queasiness. At that point I wasn't ready to leave Botswana and felt unsettled about reaching closure there.

During that time there was a Saturday morning that I particularly remember.

It was a Saturday morning like any other. Just before dawn, I stood in my yard with my morning cup of tea watching the sunrise. There was a burst of light over the eastern horizon, and then within minutes the sun blazed, silhouetting acacia trees and round mud huts in the village. The sun spilled its orange rays across the flat landscape. The burst of color and light came with a crescendo accompanied by a dawn chorus of roosters crowing, cattle lowing, and goats and dogs adding to the racket. Mourning doves in the trees kuu-ku-ku-ing.

Gen had to go to her school that Saturday — she and the other home-ec teacher at the secondary school had to cook for a sports team. I watched her pedal her bicycle out the driveway and down the paved ring road. At the place where she entered the unpaved main road she turned to wave to me.

Later that morning, I went into Francistown to buy some groceries and while I was there, I grabbed a copy of every English language newspaper I could find. By eleven, I was sitting back in my living room with a pile of newspapers and a cup of tea.

When I picked up the *Mmegi Reporter*, I became very interested in what I saw. I was looking at a hazy, slightly out-of-focus newsprint photo of a grizzled old man. His face was a gray blur in the shadow of his fedora. He wore a tattered dark jacket.

The article began, "Oom Freddy is in his nineties. The son of a Scottish immigrant who settled in Bechuanaland Protectorate and an Afrikaner woman, daughter of the Dorsland trekker family the Taljaards . . .."

I could see this man had an authentic connection to the history of Botswana. Bechuanaland Protectorate was the name of the region used on maps before its independence. Dorsland Trekkers were a group of 19th century Boers, or Dutch settlers, who crossed the Kalahari in search of better lives and lost nearly everything in the desert. This man's family had been among the survivors. I could see immediately that Oom Freddy — Oom is an Afrikaans word for uncle, or any respected older man — was connected to a past that I wanted to understand. Why did I want to learn about it? I couldn't have told you then. But the information suddenly seemed vital. It felt as though my life depended on it. And it wasn't just about history, either.

The article went on to describe Freddy's life in the Kalahari Desert where he lived with the Nharo Bushmen. The Nharo were one of the San groups and he had lived with them for seventy years.

I continued reading, but the words on the page hardly registered. My heart was pumping wildly with excitement. I realized that I no longer felt tentative and uncertain — my feelings made a sudden swing. I was no longer sitting lazily in my chair — I felt energized and alive. Something changed in me. I felt that I had a direction.

Ever since my visit to the Tsodilo Hills, I'd wondered if it would be possible to find a San group and get at least a taste of their culture. As disturbing as our interaction with the villagers there had been, the mysterious chanting near our camp at Nata had made me aware that Bushman culture had not disappeared entirely. The chanting had been a reminder that the San lived in many places around the Kalahari, not just in the village we'd visited at Tsodilo.

A jumble of questions raced through my mind.

I needed to talk with Gen.

It was nearly sunset before we had a chance to do so. As we had done many evenings, Gen and I carried a pair of kitchen chairs and two glasses of lemonade to a shady corner on our front porch. We lived in teacher housing provided by the college where I taught. Our "front porch" was actually a corner of a concrete slab extending a few feet beyond the concrete block wall of the house.

"I'd like to take a trip into the Kalahari," I began. I was trying to find a way of telling her about the news story I had read. I hadn't had time to sort through my thoughts. My mind was going in several directions. It wasn't easy to speak coherently.

Gen looked at me, puzzled. "Into the desert . . . you mean during our break?" she asked.

We had a term break coming up in a month. During that week, the Ministry of Education required all teachers to attend a conference. There was no way a trip into the Kalahari would happen then.

"When we leave our jobs at the end of the year. In January, is what I'm saying . . . .. I want to rent a truck and go places in the desert we've never been." Even as I said it, the words sounded grandiose, as if I were inviting Gen to a tropical vacationland. Actually, I was asking her to travel farther west than we had gone previously, into the Ghanzi District.

Gen had quit a good job to come to Africa with me. After two years of difficult work in a classroom, she had every right to expect a real vacation. And Gen's children lived in the US. She missed them and talked about them often. She was looking forward to getting home. I had no idea how she'd react.

I was fully aware that I was not inviting her to go on a luxury vacation. Instead of an experience of pampered comfort, there were sure to be hardships. As a substitute for a plush bed, we'd be sleeping on the ground in a tent.

"I've thought a lot about our trip to the Tsodilo Hills," I said.

Gen said, "Sure, I remember. We had a beautiful time."

"True, in a way we did. But parts of it have stayed with me — things I need to deal with. I actually felt pretty depressed about it for a while. Disillusioned might be a better word. But disillusionment seems like a way of blaming the victim and I don't want to do that." I paused and sipped my lemonade. "What I've been looking for is a way that we could experience Bushman culture. Traditional aspects, I mean."

Gen looked at me and then asked, "Do you really believe the traditions have survived? The San aren't nomads anymore."

"No, they aren't. You're right. But on the way home from Tsodilo, we camped at Nata. Remember? That night I heard a trance dance ceremony not too far from where we were in our tent."

"You mentioned it the next morning. I do remember that. I didn't hear a thing."

"I may be making assumptions, but it was a night with a full moon and there were no instruments except for rattles and hands clapping. I heard their feet stomping on the sand. And I heard several voices chanting with a leader — a shaman. By morning, even the birds were joining in. All that made me think it was a trance dance — or a healing ceremony. That's something positive I've held onto. If I'm right, it means that San culture still exists in the Kalahari. Despite the kind of despair we saw at Tsodilo, somewhere and in some form, the culture survives."

Gen smiled. "So, you're hatching a plan," she said.

I paused and was silent for a minute. I had to organize myself. "I read about a man in the newspaper today and it started me thinking. If we were to find a group of San, there would be barriers in communication, just as there were at Tsodilo. Language is a problem. But if we found someone who speaks English . . .."

"Tell me more about the man," Gen said.

I backed up. "This man lives with the Nharo — one of the Bushman groups — his father was Scottish and I assume that he must speak some English. He has lived in the desert with the Nharo for about seventy years. I'm not sure I can explain it totally, but I'd like to meet him." I put down my glass and folded my arms.

Gen's expression was non-committal. The notion of visiting someone on the basis of a news story seemed to baffle her. She thought a minute.

"So, you're interested in meeting this guy because he speaks English and lives with a Bushmen group?"

"Besides living with the Bushmen, he's in his nineties, or close to it. That means he's lived the entire 20th century." As soon as the words were out of my mouth, I realized new details that I hadn't thought of at first.

"Who knows what changes he's seen?"

"Is this a kind of historical interest then?" Gen asked.

"Historical? Not exactly. Look, he's been shaped by his experience. Living in a Nharo village is bound to affect the way a person looks at the world."

"How he looks at the world? Um hmm. Any hunches?"

"I don't know," I fumbled. "I think I'm right that the way he looks at the world is going to be unique. For starters he grew up in the desert, has a Nharo wife."

Gen waited for me to continue.

"His parents were white, yes. His father Scottish, his mother an Afrikaans speaker. I think that qualifies as a mixed marriage in this part of the world. When he was young, he took a wife . . . well outside the boundaries of his family's culture."

"Sounds like you're approaching this as a social scientist."

"I'm not a scientist . . . I'm not a historian. But there are things that make me curious and that I'd like to find out about. I'd like to know what's it like for this man."

Gen seemed to take in what I'd been saying.

She paused and said in a reflective tone, "What's it like for this man? How does he see the world?"

I'd lost the thread of my idea. I sat silently, feeling stiff and defensive, as if I were in the center of a moat.

"Know what I'm hearing?" Gen continued to push me.

"Umm?"

"You want to talk to a man. Sounds like you want to talk to a man about life. Nothing wrong with that. Other things are part of that. Belonging, for instance. That's it, isn't it?"

I hated hearing my words rephrased. It seemed to minimize everything. Wasn't it enough to be excited about meeting Freddy? Doesn't that make it important? At that moment, her words seemed to reduce everything to complicated hidden motivations. I shifted in my chair, increasingly restless.

"You've told me about the search for a father going on in your life." Gen paused. She looked off into the western sky for a minute. "How — when you were young — you used to look up to older men at your work and tried to make them into surrogates."

The deep-red sky silhouetted the buildings of the campus. My arms were folded across my chest, my legs crossed. I knew what she was saying.

The problem was that it was probably true. But hearing her say it made me uncomfortable.

My glass was empty and I used that as an excuse to retreat. With a flurry of energy, I got up from my chair and walked into the kitchen to grab a beer.

The break in our conversation gave me a chance to see things in a new light. I could see that all I had were questions at this point. I had no answers. My defensiveness was unnecessary; I knew Gen's intent was supportive. I could accept that these are parallel journeys. One is a quest, while another is a pilgrimage and part something else, maybe. It does happen. Gen was only reminding me. It was at that moment I began trying to understand what kind of journey I was on.

I opened a can of beer and went back to sit with her. We watched the sunset in silence.

4 Orwell Meets the San

Gen had reservations about an extended trip into the Kalahari. But she didn't completely dismiss the idea and so we continued to talk.

Neither of us could predict what would happen if we went into the desert, but immediately moving back to Seattle also had its uncertainties. I was trying to get used to the idea of leaving the Peace Corps, but the idea of not having a job weighed heavily on me. My unruly mind kept conjuring dramatic pictures of me unemployed in Africa. I tried to change the way I thought about it and began to think of it as a kind of creative unemployment.

Even though we were far from making a decision about the trip, I took every available opportunity to search for information about the San and how they lived. It seemed unlikely I'd find anything about Freddy, but I figured I could look and would at least find information about other travelers in the Kalahari.

Gen and I had a few days during which we could leave our jobs and travel to Gaborone so I could peruse the library at the University. Gaborone

— pronounced Hah-bor-oh-nee, but shortened to Gabs by most ex-pats — is the capital of Botswana.

In 1992, Gabs was a city of only about 200,000, but after living in a village for two years, it was easy for me to get lost there. Bustling with business and government workers, the traffic patterns were chaotic and the streets meandered like goat paths. Yet, despite the population and the traffic, there were places in the middle of the city where the pavement came to an end. I would walk off a sidewalk and find myself walking again on the red sand of Africa. Thorn bushes poked through caked soil, making the capital feel like just another African village.

In Gaborone, Gen remained quiet whenever the subject of Freddy came up or if I happened to mention the topic of traveling into the Kalahari. I knew her well enough to realize her silence wasn't reluctance. Instead she was wondering about her part of the plan: *How do I fit into this adventure? Am I just along for the ride, or do I have some purpose here?*

Our hotel was located near a market. One morning, Gen and I joined the rest of the pedestrian traffic on our way to breakfast. From the market a red sandy path headed east to the Gaborone Mall. As we walked, we became part of a crowd of people going to work. Skin colors ranged from very light to polished black. A steady press of people moved forward through parking lots, skirting office buildings and passing chain-link fences near construction sites. In the distance, familiar landmarks appeared: the microwave tower and, next to it, the 11-story, red brick Orapa House.

At the time, Orapa House must have been the tallest building in Gabs. Owned by Debswana, a partnership of the DeBeers diamond company and the Botswana government, Orapa House was where diamonds were sorted for quality.

Looking at it, I imagined inner rooms full of trays like cookie sheets covered with black felt and sparkling with icy jewels. I had a feeling that the search for diamonds and other minerals were factors leading to instability for the San.

Orapa House stood at the edge of the Gaborone Mall, near the intersection of Khama Crescent and Nelson Mandela Drive. To get through the intersection, we dodged vehicles crossing the Crescent and then headed toward the buildings that marked the Mall.

It was not yet nine o'clock when Gen and I arrived on the porch of the President Hotel, a place where we could not afford to stay, but which served an ample, reasonably-priced continental breakfast. Our table overlooked the broad brick plaza of the Mall where vendors set up their displays. As we ate, Gen read the newspaper and I watched the foot traffic in the plaza as people began their day in the city.

Across from the hotel was a three-story bank building. Glass panels faced the Mall and a wide staircase led from the front door of the bank to the plaza level. At the foot of the stairs, a woman swept the concrete with a reed broom before spreading out squares of blue vinyl. She then pulled tan leather sandals from a half dozen cardboard cartons and set them out on the plastic sheets in neat lines.

Within minutes, the six squares of plastic were covered with rows of sandals. Finishing her work, she sat on the stairs and wrapped her arms around her knees.

A few feet away from the woman, a young man set up a table of hats. On his head he wore a floppy cream-white newsboy cap. He carried a number of boxes one by one from somewhere behind the bank, and out of each he unpacked stacks of hats. When finished he had derbies, fedoras, and woolen balaclavas — apparently for days when the temperature dropped below eighty-five degrees. He had green hats, French foreign legion hats, and Australian Outback hats.

Gen set aside her paper and sighed deeply. The major stories were about violent events in South Africa connected with the ending of apartheid. "Does it seem to you that there is a civil war happening just to the south?"

The news had made me ask the same question many times. "Hard to tell, isn't it," I answered. "The massacres that have been reported make it seem like civil war. Boipatong. Bisho. The others."

The sun had moved above the buildings and the man in the floppy cap was strutting in front of his wares, chatting up passersby to call attention to his goods for sale. The plaza was now lined with tables and merchants selling kitchen implements, cassette tapes, and books. Racks of dresses and children's clothing waved in the breeze.

We finished our meal and I paid the bill. Then Gen and I began our stroll between shops toward our separate errands. Gen, carrying her sketch pad, headed to the National Museum, a low structure shaded by eucalyptus trees just a short distance from where we'd eaten. I continued east to the University of Botswana and the library, a three-story stone building on the campus.

Mid-afternoon I left the air conditioned comfort of the library reading room to follow the stairs down to the cafeteria. Inside the cafeteria there was a glare caused by sunlight reflecting off the walls of campus buildings and entering through the windows in the large room. It took a moment for my eyes to adjust. Inside, the air tasted as if vegetables had been sitting too long on the steam table. A fragrance of spiced curry mingled with the other aromas. Salad bowls piled with shredded cabbage and sliced beets were set out on a self-serve counter.

I picked up a bowl of coleslaw and a burger and then scanned the room for an empty chair. Every seat appeared to be taken, but I saw a shady spot outside a pair of double doors. Walking in that direction, I passed a group of a dozen people occupying two tables that had been pushed together. I recognized a few familiar faces, people from other colleges. I didn't know them well, only from college gatherings. There must be a meeting on campus, I thought.

At that moment, I spotted a friend. Tim Heaney saw me at the same time, stood, and waved. He and I taught at the same college. Tim, an expatriate Aussie with curly brown hair, taught social studies to prospective teachers. He had met and married an Englishwoman in Botswana before Gen and I arrived. Tim had a round face and the look of a man well fed.

Another co-worker, Esther Brooke, sat near Tim at the table. She saw me and smiled. Esther, an Englishwoman who grew up in Durban, South Africa, and graduated with a PhD from Cambridge, was tall and thin with dark hair. She wore a practical, wash-and-wear navy blue suit jacket and skirt.

I watched them disengage from their group. Both stood and excused themselves from the table and without speaking we headed toward the double doors. At the college we were usually too busy to visit, but when we did, our visits took place in the staff room during morning tea. We had a routine of stepping outdoors so Esther could smoke.

We found a small court just past the double doors. On the concrete square were two tables and some plastic chairs that had been moved there from a classroom. Despite the glare from sunlight reflected off the walls of the patio, it was a comfortable place to sit. Esther pulled a pair of aviator sunglasses from her bag.

At the college, Esther had the title of Head of Department and was often introduced as HOD Social Studies. I knew nothing about her personal life. She never discussed it and I'd never heard her mention any men in her life. I had the impression she wasn't interested in attracting men, but rather had a desire to be noticed as British. She kept her cigarettes in a flamboyant silver-tooled case that may have come from India. When we talked about academic subjects, her Cambridge accent became more pronounced, dripping from her tongue like honey and sticking to everything.

We found three chairs and once we were seated Esther immediately began to squirm on the molded plastic seat. She then held up her silver cigarette case and lighter as a kind of silent plea for understanding.

"All that secondhand smoke," she said.

Although we had moved outdoors so she could smoke, she wanted assurance and for me to convince her that I meant it. Once convinced she removed a cigarette, tapped it against the case, muttered, "Dirty habit," and lit up. It occurred to me that later in the day Gen was likely to ask why my clothing smelled like cigarette smoke.

Tim had brought his cup of tea outside with him. He held his saucer with one hand and braced his cup with the other, pushing the handle of the cup around in a circle with a pudgy finger.

"What brings you to Gabs?" I asked.

"A conference," Tim answered. "Managing the Environment. Muckymucks from the Ministry and consultants from South Africa mingling with us plain folks — social studies instructors from the teachers' colleges." Tim sipped his tea. "The Kalahari Conservation Society is paying for these luxurious digs."

Then his voice changed, indicating that the sarcasm was finished. "It's a symposium dealing with tourism, overgrazing of cattle, and government policy."

Esther blew a column of smoke into the air, "*Et vous?*"

"Gathering information on Bushmen." I didn't mention my quest to find Freddy.

"You went to Tsodilo, didn't you?" Esther asked. "I seem to remember."

"Last year."

"Sad situation there. Those people housed in a museum."

"What's going on with the Bushmen?" I asked. "Right now, I mean."

Tim enjoyed a good reputation from his lectures and articles. He talked politics with the manner of an Africa insider. He set his teacup down and shifted his plump frame to get comfortable in his chair. Right away, I knew it wasn't going to be a short answer.

"Can I take notes?" I asked.

He nodded and I pulled a pad from my pocket.

"It's the story of indigenous people all over, isn't it? Losing their culture. Pressure to assimilate. Same thing is happening to the *Basarwa*." Tim used the Setswana word Basarwa for Bushmen. "They're required to send their children to schools that stress assimilation. It's understandable; Botswana is a developing country. The Tswana — I should say the government, but they are the same thing since they are the majority of the population — need to build a sense of nationhood. But there's no doubt the Basarwa are losing out in the process."

When he talked about social issues in Botswana, it was with an air of confiding something that only "we insiders really understand."

"Assimilation policy. Then what about hunting? How can they make a living?" I asked.

"Basarwa can no longer hunt," he said. "In order to hunt, a person needs to buy a license from the government. In order to buy a license, a person needs to fill out forms printed in English. So, in effect, licensing becomes a prohibition because the typical Basarwa hunter can't read or speak English."

Tim continued. "Women can't gather food from the veld anymore. Their range is restricted because lands are fenced these days. Someone had the idea that Basarwa need to learn commercial skills. The government promotes that as an answer for everyone. It's part of economic development. In order to make a living, everyone needs to join the cash economy."

"Cash economy," I said. "I think I saw how that worked at Tsodilo. But in the desert? Is it realistic?"

"The government is filled with technocrats. This is a developing country. A developing country needs technocrats. Technocrats think everyone needs rules, so that's probably what it takes. But they have an attitude about economic development. There are obvious conflicts in land use. A nomadic culture requires territory. The priorities of the government are things like providing wildlife for tourism, making room for cattle grazing, and sponsoring mineral exploration — diamonds, oil, chemicals."

As I scribbled, I realized Tim was helping connect some pieces of the puzzle and confirming many of my observations from the Tsodilo Hills. The priorities of the developing nation don't leave room for nomadic life. The traditions of Bushmen were in conflict with the value Tswana place on cattle. Before independence in 1967, hunting was a major source of food. Now the economy depends on the sale of cattle.

Tim paused to run his hand through his curly hair and sip his tea. "In 1961, before independence, the Central Kalahari Game Reserve, an area the size of Switzerland, was gazetted for the benefit of 'wild Bushmen' hunter-gatherers."

I loved the word gazetted and wrote it down. He continued with his mini-lecture while I scribbled notes.

Tim explained that the European Community exerts an influence on the government because they're a source of exports. In the 1960s the European governments were concerned for the welfare of the Basarwa. However, in the mid-eighties, they changed their position and the Europeans voiced a strong opinion that the Central Kalahari Game Reserve should be preserved for the sole benefit of wildlife. They felt wildlife should take precedence over the Basarwa.

The change in the European attitudes suited the Ghanzi area farmers who did not want Basarwa to be given land because they used Basarwa as workers on their ranches. The labor supply disappeared if Basarwa were to move to the Central Kalahari.

Up to this point, Esther hadn't spoken. She watched Tim speak, her elbow rested against her body. The curl of smoke from her cigarette rose into the air. Finally, she exhaled noisily to signal she wanted in.

"The government always tries to appear evenhanded," she said. "They want decisions to be made without regard to racial or tribal or linguistic affiliations. Tribal groups and cattle owners are affected by decisions over the use of the Central Kalahari, not just Bushmen. Someone invented the term, RAD, to stand for Remote Area Dwellers.

"RAD! Can you believe it? Ved-dy Orwellian. The word adds a dash of tragi-comedy. The term parodies the bureaucratic decision-making. When a rule is handed down, the language doesn't have to refer to Basarwa because it applies to all RADs. Unfortunately, when translated into Setswana, the name means 'people deep within the deep.' It gives rise to all sorts of irony. Basarwa take it to mean that in the eyes of the government, they are already buried and in their graves."

I had seen the term RAD used in news accounts, but had not given much thought to its implications. A shock of recognition went through my body as I began to put together this new information. I sat forward and turned slightly toward Esther. "Okay, but are the Bushmen — Basarwa . . .?"

Esther shifted abruptly in her chair and I interrupted myself mid-question. I realized that I was acting too intense for Esther. I'd seen it before. She was embarrassed by my mannerisms. Momentarily, she looked at me as if I were about to jump on the table and flap my wings. Then a sympathetic expression crossed her face that I interpreted as, *He's only an American. He can't help it.*

It took a second for me to recover my train of thought. Scaling down my enthusiasm, I turned toward Tim and asked whether Bushmen were involved in any of the decisions.

Tim put down his cup and saucer. "Basarwa society is loosely structured; decisions are made by consensus. There's no chief and no headman. As a result, Basarwa are the losers because the whole process is political. The government discusses issues with outsiders then makes a political decision. Groups in attendance have leadership who speak for a point of view. Who is there to support the Basarwa and to fight for their rights? No one. I think it's safe to say they are often unrepresented. Consequently, decisions are made without them. But you can't always tell from reading reports."

"Yes." Esther blew a puff of smoke into the air as punctuation. "RAD policies are discussed at a meeting and who shows up? If you read accounts in the papers, all government officials are identified with proper names and titles. If a foreign representative shows up, he'll be named. Members of interest groups in attendance are acknowledged. But none of the Bushmen representatives are named in the newspaper. One exception is a man named Hardbattle — John Hardbattle — in Ghanzi. He's part Nharo himself. Owns a farm. Has an education. Hardbattle is well known and always identified. But reading a report of those meetings, you'd think he was the only person in attendance representing the Basarwa."

"And it's difficult for the Basarwa to have a single voice because they speak several different languages — related languages, but distinct," added Tim. "The result is, they're an invisible minority. The other side of the coin is, if an ordinary citizen reads a news story, how would they appreciate that the problems of Basarwa are affecting real people? News articles give no clue."

We heard a stir of voices and the sound of chairs being pushed back coming from inside the cafeteria. People were standing up and moving away from the tables for the afternoon session of the meeting Tim and Esther were attending.

The three of us stood as well. "We must get together again," Esther said, and we all agreed. We meant it, but at the college we were busy. Outside of an occasional ten-minute conversation like the one we just had, getting together was unlikely.

5 The Search

After lunch I browsed the library for books with stories about travelers in the Kalahari — men escaping from the law, people following religious prophecy, and some who were just curious. But that wasn't really what I was looking for. I remembered a book I'd seen years earlier as a college student. It had been so long ago that I was unsure whether my memory was correct. I kept looking.

I continued my search and, to my surprise, ran across several books that mentioned Freddy. One of the books was an anthropologist's survey of people living in the Kalahari. Another cited Freddy as a source in a study of useful and edible plants of the Kalahari. He was mentioned briefly in a general reference and also referred to in a quirky memoir written by a German-South African man. Freddy was described as a white Bushman. It was clear that in his ninety-five years, he had gained a reputation. People seemed to know who he was. Chances seemed better than ever that he spoke at least some English. But everything written about him was at least twenty years old. Given his age, I had a nagging question, *is he still alive?*

The newspaper article I'd read months ago in my village had said that Freddy lived with the Nharo people. The name of the group rang a bell and I thought I'd read it in a book years earlier. I was sure that if it existed, the book would be here in the University of Botswana Library. This was the mother lode of knowledge and contained everything ever written on the Kalahari.

I continued to browse.

In one small book I found a photograph. The book, written by a pair of sociologists, described a white man in the Ghanzi District who lived "openly" with his Bushman wife. The book didn't name the man, but there was a photo showing him posed with his family. The description and the circumstances fit and I suspected it was Oom Freddy, here named Freddy Morris.

The photograph depicted a classic pose: a man surrounded by family. The man sits, broad-shouldered and strong, his huge hardworking hands comfortably at rest on his lap. A wide-brimmed fedora shades his face. After a quick calculation, I estimate his age at seventy-five when the photo was taken, though he looks forty-five. His much younger Nharo wife stands to one side. Wearing a wraparound skirt, scarf tied behind her head, and an ostrich bead necklace, she holds a baby.

In the photo, two children stare back, blatantly curious about the camera and impatient with having to pose. The boy, about five years of age, stares at the camera aggressively. The girl, perhaps a year younger, leans uncertainly toward her mother. Both children look ready to resume chasing, wiggling, or wrestling.

The impressive thing about the man is his eyes. Even in the shade under the turned-down hat brim, his eyes radiate light. He seems to project a statement for the camera, the photographer, and anyone else: If you come near my family, you'll have to deal with me.

It took me another hour of searching the shelves, but I recognized it the moment I saw it. The book had a simple gray cover with the title printed in black, *The Naron*. It brought back a rush of memories.

It was the book I'd read in 1960 at the University of Washington.

I'd read the book not because I ever expected to travel into the Kalahari, but because it was thin and I was assigned a book report in my anthropology class. The author was an anthropologist named Dorothea Bleek, and she had written an ethnography of the San group still living in the Ghanzi area. The only thing that had changed in the intervening years was the spelling of the group's name: the Naron were now the Nharo — the same group Freddy lived with.

The book had been published in 1928 and reflected attitudes of the era. Bleek wrote that the lives of the Nharo people were at least partly intertwined with white settlers and, as a scientist, she was disappointed because she wanted to work with "wild Bushmen."

Although the ethnography itself was no longer of interest to me, on the same shelf with *The Naron* was a volume of Bushman stories edited by Bleek entitled, *The Mantis and his Friends: Bushman Folklore*. The stories were originally collected in South Africa by her father W. H. I. Bleek at a time when Bushmen were being systematically exterminated. Nineteenth-century European settlers in southern Africa looked upon them as sub-human, people without a culture. Bleek's father, a noted linguist and folklorist, tried to counter the prevailing view by showing evidence of a rich civilization. He transcribed myths, legends, and accounts of ritual as evidence of their unique culture. He died in 1875 and left his infant daughter, Dorothea, a large collection of unpublished folklore. Forty-eight years later, she published some of it as *The Mantis and his Friends*.

In her introduction, Bleek describes the Mantis as the "favourite hero of Bushman folklore." Bleek's work led to insights into Bushmen culture and established the Mantis as one of the trickster heroes in the world, along with the Jackal of Africa, Reynard the Fox in Europe, and, in the United States, the Raven of the Northwest Coastal Indians and the Coyote of the Plains Indians.

According to Bleek, Bushmen did not worship Mantis. Mantis was a dream Bushman; the word "dream" here means that it reflects the life of the people telling the story, in the sense that our dreams carry subliminal information about our lives. The amazing stories were portrayals of Bushman family life. In many of the stories, an unseen force threatens Mantis, bringing death and destruction to the land. Like an alien invader, the force devours everything in its path — bushes, water, wild animals, grass huts. In other tales, Mantis brings antelope into the world. He protects his creation by throwing up obstacles in the way of hunters. The stories reflected the experience of Bushmen in an arbitrary and unpredictable world. A world controlled by the whims of a trickster.

Thoughts of the Nharo and the Mantis stayed with me when I returned to the hotel. But when Gen and I met, music from a disco echoed through the halls like a jackhammer. We tried to escape to our room, but it had no adequate light for reading. Finally, we took refuge in the Pitsong Bar, a cubbyhole of a space that was nearly empty. African designs in broad abstract strokes decorated walls at either end of the room. A bartender in a white shirt worked silently wiping glasses. A lone man sat on a stool near the door. A couple of other customers talked quietly in the shadows at the far end. This was the right place to come to avoid a crowd.

At the bar we ordered two bottles of peach juice and took seats near the mirrored wall. The bartender poured our drinks from a Fruit Tree carton and set the glasses on the counter.

After paying, I turned toward a mirrored wall and caught a glimpse of a white middle-aged man. In each hand, he held a tall glass of peach juice. He looked slightly disreputable, wearing a rumpled blue shirt and trousers that could use ironing.

Returning to our table, I set the glasses down and sat. For several quiet minutes, Gen and I let events of the day flash through our minds. In my fatigue, I felt waves of uncertainty and heard voices of doubt. *Are you really doing the right thing? Wouldn't it be smarter to pack up and return to Seattle as soon as you complete your Peace Corps service? Isn't this library research just some kind of pretentious game?*

Finally, we both looked at each other and clinked our glasses. "Cheers!"

I sat back in the padded chair and let my hands feel the cool sweat on the glass. My fingers played with the drops and made lines in the moisture. After a few seconds, I glanced at Gen's black sketch pad on the table between us and studied it for a moment. She noticed me noticing it and smiled.

Gen always notes or draws everything she wants to remember in the pages of the bound book she calls her sketch pad. Its placement — prominently in the middle of our table — didn't seem accidental. I took it to be a hint about where to start our conversation.

"How was the gallery?" I asked.

"Interesting," she started to say, but the word wasn't right. She furrowed her brows, rested her chin on her hands. "Disturbing. Worthwhile."

Her hands suddenly became busy, moving across the bare table surface as if she were straightening a tablecloth. They came to rest on the cover of her sketch pad.

"Do you remember our first trip in Botswana on the way to the Tsodilo Hills? We stopped to buy baskets in a village."

"Of course . . . ." I remembered the trip, but had forgotten the part about buying baskets.

Gen was bursting to tell me something.

"It was a Tswana village. Well, today I saw baskets at the gallery. Like the ones we bought in the Kalahari. Today, I saw them differently. I saw what the women were saying about their lives — in their art — in the baskets they wove. When we were there, I didn't see what I should have been seeing. I looked at a basket and saw a souvenir. But I'll forgive myself because we hadn't been in Africa very long when we took that trip."

"Gumare," I said. "That was the village. Right?" I didn't know what she was getting at, but I could tell that it was important to her. My fingers continued to play on the side of my glass.

"That's right, Gumare. Miles from any other village. That isolated place."

"I don't understand. What did you see today?"

"I'm getting there. Just wait. I want to make sure you remember that place so you'll understand."

I took a sip and pushed back in my seat.

"In the desert. Sand everywhere. Remember the blind man shuffling through deep sand between the huts? How I wanted a photograph of the woman displaying a tall basket on her head? And the very old woman we bargained with who talked in terms of British pounds instead of pula? As if the British still controlled things and Botswana didn't have its own currency. It was all fascinating."

She paused, and then seemed to remember her juice and took a sip. "But today, I saw what I didn't see then. The women who made those baskets wove designs that say something about their lives: the mysteries and the cycles repeat from one generation to another. Things that frighten them or make them feel safe."

"Mmm . . . I'm trying to get the picture," I said. "So, you saw this in the gallery?"

"Yes. I'm getting to that. Thank you for your patience."

I made a gesture of zipping my lip.

"Okay, the gallery exhibit had two parts. Upstairs, devoted to Bushmen — including women — artists. Basarwa artists, it might be better to say."

"You mean contemporary artists painting contemporary work."

"Right, contemporary art using traditional themes. Art with images from stories of the culture. The lower half of the museum had a display of baskets. Basket weaving and designs."

"That's where you saw the baskets."

"It was all worth seeing. The baskets drew me in. I spent time in the downstairs gallery this morning and sketched. The gallery is circular and I sat in the middle." Gen glanced up at the ceiling of the bar once in a while as she spoke, as if she were seeing baskets displayed there. "From my bench, I could see everything . . . take in the whole display. Baskets all made from grasses collected in the Kalahari. Designs — as I was trying to say — more varied than I remembered. Some were startling."

She wrapped her hand around the spine of her sketch pad. "First, I looked at them. Familiar repetitive designs. Very simple, and I almost passed them by. Some of them suggest the spotted patterns of animal hides and repetitive diamonds. After a few minutes, I looked again at the first baskets and that's when — Whoa! — a few of them looked completely different the second time."

"How so?"

"It startled me. I began seeing snake skins in some designs."

"You sure?"

"I don't know if that's what the weavers saw. But the resemblance was too close to ignore. Mottled diamond design. That's when I began to feel that the design had significance other than only selling a piece of handicraft to a tourist."

"What's your idea about that?"

"I don't have an idea. But poisonous snakes have power. They pose danger and they're used in witchcraft. I don't claim any great insight here. But that is what art is supposed to do, after all. Stimulate imagination. Maybe the weaver is creating psychological protection in some way."

Gen opened her pad and flipped some pages before she found what she wanted.

"Look," she said. "Here's a design. Chicken feet. I had fun sketching this. Several baskets used it. Just three toes and a backward toe. Four simple lines, like looking at sand where chickens have walked. It's a homey farm image and works well in weaving."

In the sketch, I could see the circle of the basket with chicken feet around the side at regular intervals.

Gen turned a few pages. "Here's another. A goat design. Repeated simple images — you could call them logos. Look at them and immediately you see they're goats. All around the basket. You can't see it very well in my sketch, but it's interesting the way the design uses shade. For half the basket the goats are in dark brown. The other half they are light, sand colored. I looked at this, and then had to look again. In the use of light and dark, it's almost a depiction of day and night. Yin and yang. A portrayal of two worlds that exist simultaneously: our world — the tangible world — and the spirit world." She paged intently through more sketches before showing me another.

"Tell me, am I nuts? Am I getting too philosophical seeing all this in a basket?" Gen didn't wait for my judgment. "It blew my mind. Just sitting there, looking at baskets. I can't tell you what it did . . . those spare designs."

I sat in a comfortable slouch and listened to the energy in her voice.

"I'm not even going to begin talking about the circles they use," she said. "Concentric circles woven from darker or lighter shades of grass. Circles are probably the easiest to weave, but what is a circle? Universal image. Time. Recurring cycles like the seasons. Continuity of life. A circle is our wedding ring design."

She paused and looked around the bar for a few seconds. "Gumare," she said. "By the way, thanks for remembering the name of that place. I've been racking my brain trying to dredge that up."

"Anytime," I said. I felt more at ease in that moment than I had since coming to Gaborone. As I listened to Gen, I realized that neither of us was finished with Botswana. Gen had found her purpose. We both had questions and more to learn in Africa.

"When we were in Gumare, I didn't know how to understand what I was seeing. With my limited understanding, I saw what I was prepared to see. A picture of quaint village life under extreme conditions."

"Amazing," I said. "I think I know what you mean."

I looked around; the bar was still nearly empty. A man sat alone, the same fellow that was there when we entered and he hadn't moved since. Three pint glasses sat on the counter surface in front of him; two were empty. He slumped on his elbows, nearly asleep on the barstool.

We left the bar and walked up the stairs. Between the second and third floors, two women hefted a large chrome floor polishing machine to the next level. Three others in dresses of sky-blue cotton worked on their hands and knees to spread a thick coat of wax. The loud hum of a buffing machine echoed through the tiled corridor.

As we rounded a corner on the stairs between the third and fourth floor another group of women in blue dresses sat in the narrow passageway chatting and sharing segments of an orange. Two women stood and curtsied in mock deference. "Dumela, sir," they said. I nodded a weary greeting. We smiled and squeezed past.

Walking down the long fourth floor corridor on the way to our room, I watched a large beetle struggle to cross the hall on the freshly waxed, highly polished surface. He started out in one direction, and then lost his footing. He regained his balance and headed off toward another destination. I thought of picking him up and scooting him along, but I had no way of knowing where he wanted to go. I shrugged. *Did I know where I wanted to go?* I heard a voice somewhere in my mind: *No one's going to carry you. You'll have to find your own direction.*

I was reminded of the photo I'd seen in the library — I was sure it was Freddy. The way his eyes burned: steady, strong, challenging. Doubts or uncertainty? I don't think so. If he had either, he'd dealt with it and moved on. The way his eyes shone under the broad dark brim of the fedora answered my question.

Something told me that long ago, he'd made a decision. In doing so, he'd been able to cross a boundary. He'd broken rules. Yet he seemed to thrive. I wanted to know how it impacted him. What other decisions had he made?

More than ever, I wanted to know his story.

Gen's insights about the basket designs still reverberated and I let the thought about Freddy echo through my mind for a minute. *Yes, that's true,* I thought finally. *I do want to know his story, but maybe that's another way of saying that there's a lot more I want to learn before I go home.*

6 On the Train

Our final school year in Botswana ended in December, about a month after Gen and I talked in the Pitsong Bar. We had agreed that we wanted to conclude our stay there with a trip into the Kalahari — we were going to try to find Freddy Morris. We said our good-byes in the village and traveled to Gaborone to complete the paperwork that officially ended our Peace Corps service. Finishing our errands in Gaborone, we set out to catch the morning train to Francistown, the next town on the way, and where we had made arrangements to rent a white-canopied truck called a *bakkie*.

In the train station a uniformed man in a billed cap patrolled the waiting room. He used a computer device the size of a notepad to issue train tickets. He took my money and printed out one ticket before the machine stopped working. The man wrinkled his brow, punched some keys, but nothing happened. Handing me the one ticket and change, he told me to buy the other ticket on the train.

We found seats in the last car of economy class, and in a few minutes the train lurched north. Once we were underway, I became very thirsty. I found a drinking fountain in a shadowy corner at one end of our car. It was a modern, wall-mounted, stainless steel, refrigerated water dispenser, but when I pressed the button, it shot out a stream of warm liquid that smelled like refrigeration gas. I didn't drink it.

I looked back at Gen still in her seat. She had a book open and seemed deeply involved in reading. So, without saying anything, I walked two cars forward to buy a cup of tea at the kitchen. Behind the service window a young man slumped on a stool, his head propped in his hands and his face shaded by a red baseball cap. Near his right elbow was a small box holding cellophane bags of potato chips. I asked for tea and he appeared to understand, but looked confused. He stammered, but couldn't find the words to respond. I rephrased my request in Setswana.

"Finished," he finally told me.

Finished? The train had barely left the station. I knew he could not be out of tea. "*Feditse?* Finished? *Ga o na le te?* You have no tea?" I tried to say it in as many ways as I could.

"Yes," he said. "No hot." He pointed at the corner of his small cubicle. There was an empty spot on the orange Formica workspace where the hot plate should have been. It was missing, maybe stolen. He had no way to heat water.

"*A o na le* Pepsi?" Do you have Pepsi?

"Ehe, I have." He reached into a carton on the floor and placed a bottle on the counter. Warm as toast.

"Cold? Can I have a cold one?" I stumbled with the language and it struck me that I'd lived in Botswana over two years without learning the word for "cold." I pointed to the refrigerator behind the counter.

"*Nyaa, rra.* Fridgy finished." The refrigerator didn't work.

I couldn't convince myself to drink a warm Pepsi. It made me think of an antidote for some kind of stomach condition. Sour tummy, maybe. I walked as far forward as I could go, to a car at the head of the train, and picked out an empty seat on an orange vinyl bench. I watched the landscape move past, felt the clickety-clickety motion, and let rhythmic vibrations stir childhood memories of travel. Despite the inconveniences, going on a journey gave me a deeply pleasurable sensation. There was no continuity to my thoughts, only the pleasure of going somewhere.

Then I got up and moved through the cars, occasionally occupying an unused seat or looking out a window. The rains had returned after a two-year drought. Lush tall grass and fields green with crops lined both sides of the track. Well-fed cattle grazed in unfenced grassland. The last time I'd traveled here, the land looked dead, everything sparse and dry.

The threat of drought is always present in Botswana. Weather is a constant topic of conversation. Rain often seems like a chance event and can be very localized. Though rains had returned in the south, farmers in the north were still waiting for the drought to end. There, as all farmers in Botswana do, they watch for signs.

During the drought, on a day that clouds had gathered, a cattle owner in my village had told me about the signs of rain.

"Rain will come," he said. "Did you hear the *senyetse* last night?" Senyetse were huge flies, the size of a fifty-cent piece. They gathered by the hundreds on leaves and branches screeching like chainsaws outside my bedroom window.

I'd heard them, of course. During the night a lot of them died and in the morning they crunched underfoot.

"The insects are a good sign," he told me.

On another day we had clouds and lightning and it looked like rain, but a downpour failed to materialize. "We almost had it," he said. "Just too much lightning."

The Setswana word for rain, pula, also means luck. In Botswana, the currency is also called pula. Rain, luck, money — all of them are unpredictable, and all of them add up to one's fortune in life. As Gen and I rode the train north that morning, our fortune lay before us. It looked favorable. The unusually green landscape and fat cattle in the fields were good signs.

I wandered the train for about an hour and then returned to the car where Gen sat, and found her having a conversation with an American woman I recognized. I'd seen her at the Peace Corps office, but we'd never spoken. I knew she was a teacher, but I didn't know her name.

I heard the woman say, ". . . and he just dumped me."

"Ooh, that's too bad," Gen said. I decided not to sit too close. Gen has an ability to draw people out. Strangers tell her things about their lives they wouldn't tell anyone else.

I found an empty seat three rows back where I couldn't hear the conversation. Even sitting there, I could hear Gen's occasional sympathetic noises.

At one point, the train slowed. Maintenance was being done on the track bed. A crew of a dozen railroad workers in orange overalls leaned on shovels near piles of crushed rock. I looked out the window, beyond the rock pile, where I caught a glimpse of a sandy road just east of the track.

The road was visible in some places from the train. About a quarter of a mile from the railroad track, it stretched north and south. I recognized it as the road that passed through our village, the road everyone referred to as the "main road."

Never maintained, it was perilous to drive, but during our two years there it became my favorite place to walk in the afternoons. In the nineteenth century, it used to be known as Missionary Road. David Livingstone and others followed the road into the interior of Africa. The Boers and Tswana fought a vicious territorial war because Boers wanted it to be the boundary between the Transvaal of South Africa and what was then called Bechuanaland. In the 1890s, the Tswana granted land parallel to Missionary Road for Cecil Rhodes — of Rhodes Scholar fame and the richest man in the world at the time — to use in building a railroad to Bulawayo, in current-day Zimbabwe. Our train to Francistown traveled on modern track, but it followed the same route where Rhodes laid his track.

When we finally arrived at the train station on Haskins Street in Francistown, my watch said 1:15 p.m. An employee of the rental agency had brought the bakkie to the station, which was opposite the crowded African Market. We spotted the truck parked in front of the colorful stalls, a throng of people were leaning against it. Hertz–Safari Class was printed on the door in yellow letters. The agent held a clipboard with white, yellow, and pink forms for us to sign. After filling them out, the people moved away from the truck and we drove the agent three blocks to her office on Blue Jacket Street.

I was happy to see a thirty-gallon jerry can for drinking water in the back of the bakkie. There were also built-in tanks over the rear wheels for carrying wash water. Sweet drinking water would be at a premium beyond Francistown, and we needed to carry a sufficient amount. Water available to us in desert villages and towns would be saline.

The Kalahari Desert was once a series of lakes, but when the geology changed they dried up leaving a vast beach with deep sand and very little water, which is, of course, of great concern for travelers. Rain does fall, but even in a good year when there is nine inches of precipitation, there is no drinkable surface water. Vegetation captures some of the rain, while sand sucks up the rest. David Livingstone was able to make a successful crossing in 1849 only because local people guided him to waterholes.

Before we left town, one of my tasks was to fill the jerry can.

Besides water, my other concern was fuel. As far as I knew, our only chances to refuel the truck would be in Maun and Ghanzi. From Francistown to Maun we'd be traveling a distance of roughly 300 miles. The two fuel tanks in the truck held a capacity of 230 liters of petrol, about 61 gallons. If the truck's gas mileage was at least ten miles per gallon, we should have half a tank by the time we arrived in Maun.

7 Circling of Storks

We didn't plan to go far on our first day of driving. We left Francistown late in the afternoon and, after thirty miles of paved highway, turned off a side road into the village of Sebina. Our friend Marjorie, who'd traveled with us to the Tsodilo Hills, lived in Sebina and had invited us to spend the night.

At the turnoff into Sebina, tall umbrella thorn trees shaded an area where people waited for rides. Buses stopped there taking passengers north, south, or east. We followed a road that led through the village past gently rolling hills.

Gen and I pitched our tent in Marjorie's front yard and then waited for her to come home from the school where she taught. That evening, we threw together ingredients for dinner. I grabbed a cabbage and a jar of peanut butter from the truck. Marjorie contributed spaghetti noodles and African hot sauce. When it was ready to be served it made quite a mess on the plates. But we chose to think of it as a pad thai dinner. It was certainly the best Thai food I'd had in Botswana. We shared a can of beer three ways and, after dinner, sat around the kitchen table and talked late into the night.

Marjorie asked about our trip and I described what I knew about Freddy.

"Members of his mother's family had been part of a group of Afrikaners known as the Dorsland Trekkers, who crossed the Kalahari Desert in the late 1870s. The family then farmed and raised cattle in the Ghanzi area for two or three generations. From the little I know," I continued, "Freddy seems to have been on his own trek. He's gone in a direction very different from that of his ancestors. He grew up in the community of Afrikaners around Ghanzi, yet he has lived his life with Bushmen. It takes a special kind of person to jump from one culture to another."

Marjorie asked, "He's living with the Bushman group now? That must have posed a challenge."

"Apparently he was ostracized for years by his white neighbors."

Gen added, "He stood up to the community, though. Made his decision and stuck to it."

"I don't know all the details," I said. "I doubt it was a decision based on morality, politics, or anything like that. It makes me curious."

Marjorie asked, "Any idea how old this man is?"

"Pretty old," Gen said.

"Yeah, pretty old," I said. "No way of knowing exactly. The newspaper said he was in his nineties. That would make him about the same age my father would be, I think. Within a year or so, anyway."

"So, where exactly does this man live?" Marjorie asked.

"Good question. We don't know. Somewhere in the Ghanzi District."

She laughed. "That's a huge area. Could be anywhere in the western Kalahari, clear to Namibia."

"I know," I said. "Maybe we're looking for the proverbial needle in a haystack."

In the morning Marjorie had to leave for school, but the three of us had time for a quick breakfast. We sat around her table and could see out the kitchen window. Clouds had moved in overnight making the sky a dull slate gray. We sipped tea and watched as a flight of storks came flying low. Hundreds of the huge birds circled, gliding effortlessly, wings barely moving.

"Isn't it funny," Marjorie said. "They fly so high they can't be seen. Then they simply appear . . . out of nowhere."

I took a sip of my tea but it was a little too hot. "Something brings them. Wet weather might bring a hatch of insects. Maybe plump toads have been hibernating underground and will crawl out if it rains."

"Mysteries of the stork." Gen had a dreamy, far off expression.

"Storks are a sign of rain," Marjorie said. "That's what the villagers say. We haven't had rain for two years."

"Two years, wow," I said. "Storks are a good sign then."

"Farmers will appreciate it." Marjorie held her mug close to her face with both hands. Her words echoed from the bottom of the cup.

The mass of birds showed different patterns of white and black markings under the wings. "It's amazing," I said. "Hundreds of birds. Yet, they seem remarkably quiet."

In fact, the birds were silent. It was hypnotic watching them fly in a gradually descending line to land in the fields.

Marjorie jerked herself to attention. Setting her cup on the table with a thump, she rose and then, with hugs all around, walked out the door.

Gen and I set to work repacking the truck in preparation for our drive to Nata.

8 Into the Desert

The sky became darker as we drove to rejoin the highway. By the time we passed the bus stop under the canopy of thorn trees, rain had started to fall and large drops made muddy red splotches in the dust on our windshield.

I made the turn toward the northwest. Miles ahead, I could see a sharp line in the sky where the bank of clouds ended. Within fifteen minutes of driving, the weather changed. The sky became blue, the sun bright and hot.

As we drove, fine white sand began drifting across the highway. Plants were soft muted browns or greens, the landscape a colorless gray monotone. Trees gave way to low thorn bushes and grass, as the bushveld gradually changed to grassland.

Until sometime in the 1980s, the highway we were driving on had been an unpaved road. In Botswana, government officials are fond of telling the story that when the British left, granting the country its independence in 1966, the young nation had less than ten miles of paved highway. Yet, by not paving the road, the British unintentionally preserved Botswana. Europeans — except for miscellaneous ivory traders, explorers, or religious zealots — did not want to travel there. The stability of Botswana as a nation may be due to the fact that Europeans didn't meddle to the extent that colonial countries did in other mineral rich areas of Africa.

The same principle of cultural preservation applies to the San. Their life today would be much less disrupted if valuable minerals had not been discovered. First it was diamonds, found shortly after independence. Later, the government decided to make the most of the phosphates and other minerals provided by the desert environment. Until then, Kalahari Bushmen had retained their traditional way of life in large areas. Explorers seeking oil, diamonds, or minerals arrived in four-wheel-drive Jeeps and Land Rovers. Likewise, cattle growers and wealthy game hunters moved in. The nomadic San had no chance when the modern world began to encroach.

We'd been driving for about forty minutes when we came to a mandatory stop at a veterinary fence. The fence crosses the desert from the highway we were on to the border of Namibia and a gate barricades the highway. The fence was built to stop the huge migrations of animals that once roamed from South Africa into Zambia. Cattle owners, fearing the spread of hoof and mouth disease, wanted to prevent contact between wild animals and domestic cattle. At the gate, all drivers must stop and answer one question: Are you carrying any meat or animals in your vehicle?

We answered "No."

The gate was lifted and we drove on.

Although the highway was not perfectly straight, it was straight enough to bring on a case of boredom. I made up a game of counting microwave towers. Towers were spaced at intervals of twenty-five miles. For long stretches of the highway, the towers and the road itself were the only human marks on the flat landscape.

Before the towers were built, it was the baobab trees that were the landmarks. They attain heights of over a hundred feet, with trunks up to thirty feet in diameter at their base. With their fleshy bark that sags and wrinkles and their thick arm-like branches that reach out with gnarled fingers, each baobab has a distinct personality. Like the trees in a magical forest, you can't help but expect them to move around. Every few miles we passed one of these lone giants along our route.

The distance Gen and I drove in two hours on the paved highway took David Livingstone two weeks in 1850 with his wagon drawn by oxen. In the 1870s, Freddy Morris's grandparents must have traveled months to cross the desert with the Dorsland Trekkers. The trekkers in that group followed a vision they thought to be biblical prophecy. They believed they were heading into a paradise preordained in the Bible, where white-skinned people would rule over the natives. They managed to cross the desert, but in the process they lost half their people and most of their animals.

Driving deeper into the desert, I became increasingly aware of the sand — the fine grains blew constantly across the pavement, often blurring the boundary between what belongs to the creatures of the desert and what belongs to the humans. Occasionally small cyclones gathered and sent the weightless particles twisting high into the air.

As we drove, we saw a dozen ostrich running ahead. The flock paused to watch our truck go past. They appeared to be waiting for the desert to reclaim what was rightfully theirs.

We had been driving three hours when we arrived at Nata Lodge that afternoon. This was the same lodge we had camped at during our trip to the Tsodilo Hills. The air felt remarkably humid considering our location in the desert.

Five miles beyond the lodge there is a major junction where the main highway leads north to Victoria Falls, Zambia, or into Central Africa, and the other road heads west and deeper into the Kalahari — this was the road Gen and I planned to take.

For the next few days, we would stay at the lodge. Gen wanted a pause to allow her time for sketching. I needed time to study the notes I'd gathered at the University library.

As I was setting up our tent in the camping area, I remembered the trance dance ceremony. Since we were here, I thought about trying to find where the dance took place. After making camp, Gen headed to the bird-feeding trays in the outdoor restaurant to sketch. I read my notes for a while and then went for a walk.

The western sky was a deep coral red by the time Gen and I took a table in the open-air bar under a thatch roof. The air was still hot and muggy. We'd made plans to meet a friend later, but we had time for dinner before he arrived. We sat at a table near the thick base of a morula tree that ruled over the courtyard in daylight and loomed in the shadows at night.

"A sit down dinner," Gen said. "I'd better enjoy it. Won't happen again for a while."

In honor of the occasion, she had dressed up. Gen looked quite pretty in her pink blouse, necklace, and blue African-print knee-length shorts. I felt a bit shopworn by comparison. I'd worn the same blue shirt and khaki trousers since we left Francistown.

While we waited for the server to take our orders, I said, "I think I found the place where the trance dance was held."

Gen looked bewildered. "What trance dance?"

"Remember? I told you about it. When we were here with Jim and Marjorie?"

"I remember that, but not the part about the trance dance."

I laughed. "Well, you were asleep. Why should you remember? I was the one who was awake."

Our waitress chose that moment to bring us water and silverware. After she had set everything down and taken our orders, I continued. "This afternoon, I followed a trail through the brush and found the place. Over behind those bushes . . . ."

I pointed it out, although the light was too dim to see details. "The sand is hard-packed and there's an enclosure with a thatch roof supported by several poles. Antelope antlers are mounted on the poles and it has a fire pit in the center. Certainly looks like a ceremonial spot."

Gen listened politely and then we sat silently. For a few minutes, neither of us knew what to talk about. It was one of those times when Gen and I seemed to occupy separate worlds. At that moment, I realized I'd prefer to be cooking out in the desert, rather than waiting for a meal in a restaurant. I looked forward to camping for the next several days, sitting together with Gen in the sand, shoulder-to-shoulder or knee-to-knee, where we could share food and eat with our fingers. This restaurant wasn't really formal, but someone else defined our space with a place setting. We had to follow the etiquette of ordering our meal and then waiting for someone to bring our portions.

The waitress returned with a glass of diet Pepsi. I hadn't taken more than a few sips, when moths the size of sparrows flew into the bar from bushes nearby. Several landed on tables around us. One took a liking to my soft drink. He landed on the rim and his brown spotted wings covered the glass entirely. Then he moved slowly around the rim where a few sugary drops clung to the glass. His long tongue uncurled, either to lap up or suck like a straw, I didn't know which.

"Is this thing making love to my glass?" I asked.

Gen laughed.

I watched out of curiosity and interest, but after a few minutes I lost patience. Finally, I shooed him away.

Our laughter attracted the attention of the people at the next table.

"Phane moth," one of the men said. I hadn't noticed the group until the man spoke to us. He, another man, and a woman — remnants of a larger group — were finishing up their meal. Two tables had been pushed together for a party of six. Plates, glasses, and crumpled napkins remained where the rest of the party had gathered earlier.

"Apparently emerged from a cocoon nearby," the man continued. He wore a bush suit, the kind of sage-green cotton shirt and trousers that a naturalist or safari guide might wear. He smiled as he spoke and I liked him immediately. There was something about the way he spoke that made me think he might be a scientist.

"Are you a naturalist?" I asked him.

"No," he said. "I am part of a team on a contract with the government. We have driven from Nairobi to make a report on tourism and conduct a study on problems with certain game animals."

I wanted to ask more about his work, but we were interrupted when the waitress brought our dinner — two hamburgers and a Greek salad. She set a burger in front of each of us and the salad between us to share.

I speared a cube of feta cheese and an olive with my fork. Gen used the rounded edges of her spoon to go digging after a slice of tomato at the plate's edge. Before long, I became aware that we were being watched. The woman at the next table glanced toward us with an expression that seemed both shy and receptive, while the two men appeared to be sharing a secret joke.

I thought I knew what the joke might be about. In Africa, people often will say, "They eat from the same pot" as a way of describing a couple. There we were, picking bites from the plate that sat between us, sharing the same pot.

The man from Nairobi sat quietly for a few minutes. Then, after a few joking comments about the moths, he resumed our earlier conversation from his table.

"You asked if I was a naturalist. Actually, I am a doctor of veterinary medicine. A wildlife veterinarian," he told me. "I am here to inspect the health of an antelope herd in the southwest part of the country. The herd appears to be diminishing in size."

He explained that others in the team were prepared to work with Bushmen to train them as tourism guides and camel drivers to carry tourists into game parks. The team would also make recommendations for modernizing tourist accommodations.

We didn't have a long conversation. Everyone at his table had finished their dinner and soon they got up to leave.

On the other side of the bar, a chorus of voices roared excitedly. Moths were flying around the tables and for a few moments everyone in the restaurant seemed simultaneously annoyed and amused by the invaders. As darkness settled, however, we found that we had allies in the large tree a few feet from where we sat. With nightfall, a family of bush babies was becoming more active in the branches.

Their glowing yellow eyes peered out from a small platform on the side of the tree trunk. As we stared into the darkness, more eyes appeared. Bush babies are tiny nocturnal primates able to jump five or six feet vertically from a flat-footed stance to branches higher in the tree. Like owls, they have the ability to move their heads around almost completely.

"I need a picture of this." Gen leaped up to retrieve her camera from the truck. When she returned, I held a flashlight while she took photos.

The huge moths continued to fly around the restaurant, and as Gen looked through the viewfinder of her camera, we heard crunching noises. The crunching was the sound made by the bush babies as they caught moths and devoured them up in the tree. In the beam of light, we watched the family take fruit from the platform left by the owners of the restaurant, pick gum from the bark of the tree, and snag moths in midair. It was their version of a three-course meal.

We'd finished our dinner by the time our friend Jeff arrived. We saw Jeff infrequently and it was a treat when we did get together. To celebrate, all of us ordered Irish coffee.

In the US, Jeff had been a contractor and now he was responsible for developing a wildlife sanctuary a few miles from the lodge on the edge of the Makgadikgadi Pans. The lettering on his green-billed hat read Kalahari Conservation Society and his face was tanned from working outdoors. His crews built cabins, developed trails, and fenced the preserve. Formerly a Peace Corps Volunteer, he'd taught at a school in Nata and had lived in the village for years. We had some catching up to do, and, at first, our conversation focused on news about mutual acquaintances. Jeff's work with local crews gave him some knowledge about the tribal makeup around Nata. Since, I was still trying to satisfy my lingering curiosity about the trance dance, I steered the conversation to a new subject and asked, "Are there Bushmen living around here?"

"Nata was originally a Basarwa village," he said in his Missouri drawl. "Now, it's mostly a mixture of Tswana and Kalanga." The Kalanga are a minority tribal group.

"What about your crew?" I asked. "Are the men Basarwa?"

"The crew's a mixture," Jeff answered. "Some of the men are treated like Basarwa in the village. Villagers call them Basarwa. But I really can't tell the difference between them and Kalanga. Intermarriage, I guess."

"Are there still remnants of the culture, even if you can't see physical differences?" I asked.

Jeff hesitated. "What I see are differences in roles, like a caste system, maybe. Typically, Basarwa become serfs of the Kalanga."

"That sounds like what I saw at the Tsodilo Hills," I said. "A feudal relationship. I had to pay an Humbukush headman in order for a Dzu Twasi man to give us a tour."

"It takes different forms," Jeff said. "Here, the Basarwa oversee cattle posts. Instead of wages, they get food and shelter. It takes another form in the marriage patterns. Kalanga men can marry Basarwa women, but it doesn't work the other way around. Kalanga women almost never marry Basarwa men. There's a saying that the women are Motswana, but the men are Masarwa." Jeff used singular forms of tribal names. "That describes the way that the Basarwa are being assimilated into the larger society through intermarriage. Women marry outside the Basarwa group, but men don't have that option because of their lower status."

Our cups sat empty on the table. I asked if anyone wanted a second round. Jeff demurred because of work the next day.

He leaned back comfortably and, lifting his cap, ran his hand over the top of his hair. "You've heard the story that the first president of Botswana was the son of a Basarwa concubine."

"Sir Seretse Khama?" Gen asked. "I hadn't heard. Had you?" She looked at me.

"No," I said. "I didn't know that."

Jeff continued, "Seretse was taken away from his mother at a young age and grew up never knowing her. You hear people whisper the story as gossip, but no one's really surprised or shocked. In a way, the story describes the relationship between Basarwa and other groups in Botswana. They have a lower position on the totem pole, I guess you could say. But in a way that's hard to explain, there's still a deep respect towards them."

We'd been talking for over two hours when Jeff looked at his watch. The restaurant was nearly empty. "Well, work tomorrow and I have a long drive. Picking up supplies in Francistown."

As he rose from his chair, Jeff asked, "What are your plans? In Nata, I mean."

I told him we were going to visit the pans the next day.

The pans are depressions in the Kalahari where the accumulation of salts and calcium have formed a hard surface. Water collects there and it's a wonderful place for observing wildlife.

"We've been developing sites for bird watching," he said. "There's quite a bit of water this year. You should see lots of birds. Enjoy!"

9 In the Pans

We waved good-night to Jeff and walked back to our campsite. When we arrived, I was disappointed to see that two men had made camp in an adjacent spot and they had parked their small pickup truck, stacked high with construction equipment, a little too close to us. They'd built a bonfire in the brick fireplace, and as I walked past I saw that one of the men was tending to two large slabs of meat cooking on a grill over the fire while his friend reached under the seat inside the vehicle and pulled out two green pint bottles of J&B scotch.

Gen and I sauntered around the campground for an hour or so, and when we returned, our neighbors were laughing raucously and carrying on a loud conversation in Afrikaans.

Sometime during the night I woke up with a start to what sounded like the roaring of a lion. Suddenly alert, I sat up. Only when I was fully awake did I realize the noise was the sound of the two men snoring in the next tent.

The next morning I had trouble waking up. Even though it was early, the air was muggy and much too hot. In my groggy state, my head felt thick.

Our camping neighbors were still snoring in their tent.

It reminded me of when I overslept as a child on summer vacation I would hear my father's snores in the next room. During World War II, he usually worked a late shift in the shipyard and came home from work after midnight, his lungs full of smoke and fumes from crawling through the unventilated bilge of a naval ship. Before going to bed, he poured himself a shot of bourbon as a remedy for the poison he had inhaled and when he got up, his breath smelled of whiskey.

I dressed and crawled out of the tent. Bracing myself, I tried to stand, but I'd placed the tent too close to a thorn bush. My shirt got snagged on a branch and it held me down. I managed to get untangled, and then tripped on a rock.

Gen got up soon afterwards, gathered our laundry, and took it to a washing machine. When she returned, we made our way to an outdoor table at the restaurant where I ordered a pot of tea. When it arrived, it tasted salty. I added sugar and cream, but that didn't help. The taste of the tea influenced everything else. Two slices of toast also tasted as if they had been salted heavily. Gen ordered a boiled egg. She ate hurriedly and then disappeared to check on the laundry.

After she left, I asked the waitress to bring me an egg. I hardly ever eat boiled eggs at home, but when I do, I like the yolk slightly cooked. In Botswana, at an elevation of 3,000 feet above sea level, I was never sure how to order the perfect boiled egg. How should it be timed? Four minutes, four and a half, or five? Within a few minutes a boiled egg arrived in a neat white eggcup. I tapped the shell with my spoon around the rim of the small porcelain cup, and within seconds, egg white and yolk began to ooze out over the sides.

Under cooked.

Picking fragments of eggshell out of my breakfast, I looked up when the owner of the lodge came up behind me.

"Th'yig aw'right?" he asked.

He startled me, and at first I didn't understand what he had said. He was a stout Rhodesian who seemed to be in constant motion around the lodge. Passing through the restaurant, he had a plumbing wrench in one hand and a plate of fruit and birdseed in the other. Apparently he noticed me having difficulty.

I replied with a mumbled, "No problem, really."

"Sindit back," he said.

I assured him it would be fine once I picked out the shells. He went on his way, and I took a sip of saltwater tea.

It was mid-morning when we left the lodge to go to the pans.

The entrance to the sanctuary was guarded by large baobab near the gate. Beyond the gate, we drove on an unpaved sand track for about a mile or two west to the Makgadikgadi Pans. Where the road was dry, it was wash-boarded — or "corrugated" as they say in Botswana. Recent rains had left much of the track soft and boggy.

I drove at a moderate speed as we watched for wildlife. Our truck groaned, croaked, and bumped along, rocking painfully and complaining loudly. At a fork, I took the left branch.

"Let's go to the lookout point first," I said. There were several lookout points, but one had a tall wooden structure that would allow us to see farther.

The track passed several small pans where birds clustered around the edge of an alkaline pond. Sacred ibis, large white birds with curved black beaks, foraged in the tall grass for insects and small amphibians.

In places, the road surface formed a crust and our tires made popping noises as they broke through. At other spots, the road became smooth and the tires whined in the sand.

Some plover-type birds showed their heads in the tawny brown grass on either side of the road. I stopped and we got out to stretch our legs. Knee-high grass grew in dry brown clumps. The dry grass formed spikes that stabbed at our legs and feet wherever we walked. When we climbed back into the truck, we were elevated enough that we could see the white glare of water in the distance.

Further on I slowed and then stopped. "Ostrich," I said, pointing at dark clumps in the distance. They looked like shrubs until they moved and shifted position. Gen reached into a small pack on the floor for her binoculars.

We rolled forward, and Gen called out, "Springbok!"

A small herd of cinnamon-brown antelope grazed on one side of the road. Their ribbed horns curved gracefully. I stopped the truck twenty-five yards away from them. Once in a while an animal raised its white face to look at us looking at them. Their tails worked constantly slapping at their flanks.

As we approached the shore of the large pan, a straight line extended across the horizon from south to north. The flatness was astonishing. It was a view of the earth that I had seen nowhere else except at the ocean.

These pans, flat and alkaline, occupy the center of the desert and the surface hardens to a kind of concrete because of soluble minerals — calcium, salts, nitrates that precipitate as the water evaporates. A white scum rims the pans and during dry periods they gleam and produce a blinding white glare in the desert sun.

The road we followed took a bend to the south and followed the shore, where thousands of birds fed in the water. There were white pelicans, spoonbills, herons, and cranes. About a mile south, we could see a mass of pink. The color was unmistakable. A flock of flamingoes lined up along the shore. I kept the truck at a crawl, so as not to frighten the birds, until we came to the base of the tower, where I stopped. The tower was a square structure built out of treated wood, like decking lumber, with two elevated platforms. One platform was at twelve feet and the other was twenty feet above the ground. We got out and climbed the ladder to the top.

The vastness of the pans made me feel lost in time — alone and small. I was reminded of a beetle I'd seen at the Gaborone Hotel, slipping and sliding on the polished floor. Standing on the edge of the pans, I was the size of a bug on its journey down a long hallway. In this place with no landmarks, I was reminded of how much I rely on signposts for direction. If someone put me down in the middle of this vast space, how would I know which way to go?

In the mid-nineteenth century, when Livingstone traveled through this region, it was a struggle to find water, not only for men but for wild animals as well. In his account of his exploration, Livingstone tells of herds of zebra, gnu, and buffalo that stood for days, looking wistfully toward the wells for a share of the nasty water. It was the only water available, but it was also where the Bushmen waited in ambush.

In his book *Missionary Travels and Researches in South Africa*, Livingston wrote that, "In desperation they come slowly up to drink in spite of the danger, 'I must drink, though I die.' The ostrich, even when not wounded, cannot, with all his wariness, resist the excessive desire to slake his burning thirst . . .."

On his journey to Lake Ngami in 1850, Livingstone's party became lost. He wrote that a member of the group on horseback saw a Bushman woman ". . . running away in a bent position, in order to escape observation." At first, the man thought he was seeing a lion and gave chase. When he galloped up to her, "she thought herself captured and began to deliver up her poor little property, a few traps made of cords; but, when I explained that we only wanted water, and would pay her if she led us to it, she consented to conduct us to a spring. It was then late in the afternoon, but she walked briskly before our horses for eight miles . . . . After leading us to the water, she wished to go away home . . ., but as it was now dark, we wished her to remain. As she believed herself still a captive, we thought she might slip away by night; so, in order that she should not go away with the impression that we were dishonest, we gave her a piece of meat and a good large bunch of beads; at the sight of the latter she burst into a merry laugh, and remained without suspicion."

Livingstone stopped at a watering hole called Orapa, seventy miles southwest as the flamingo flies — on the opposite side of the pan from the wooden tower where I stood. Nowadays, Orapa is off limits to travelers. Only people having business with the diamond industry may go there. In the 1850s, however, diamonds had not been discovered.

On February 8, 1853, Livingstone wrote that, "great flats all around we saw in the white sultry glare. We passed the small well named Orapa . . . its water is salt and purgative . . .. Here the bulb of the thermometer, placed two inches beneath the soil, stood at 128 Deg . . .. The water . . . was bitter, and presented indications not to be mistaken of having passed through animal systems before. All these waters contain nitrates, which stimulate the kidneys and increase the thirst. The fresh additions of water required in cooking meat, each imparting its own portion of salt, make one grumble at the cook for putting too much seasoning in, while in fact he has put in none at all, except that contained in the water. Of bitter, bad, disgusting waters I have drunk not a few nauseous draughts; you may try alum, vitriol, boiling, etc., etc., to convince yourself that you are not more stupid than travelers you will meet at home, but the ammonia and other salts are there still; and the only remedy is to get away as quickly as possible to the north."

As Gen and I lingered on the tower by the edge of the pans, watching the flamingoes just two hundred yards away. A thousand of them formed a line near the shore, the long-legged birds performing a kind of dance as they fed on briny shrimp and insects. In constant motion, the birds dipped and stepped. Their beaks made a clatter. Occasionally, something startled them and the entire flock rose forming a line in the sky. Eventually, the line spiraled lower and the birds settled again in the same spot in the shallow salty water to resume their feeding dance.

Even after climbing down from the tower, we didn't leave right away. Instead, we sat on a low bank near the edge of the pan. Sweat dripped from my forehead, my hat was soaked. I took it off and hung it over a hummock of stiff grass while we continued to watch the great flocks of birds feeding along the shore. Completely relaxed and without a care in the world, I felt the tug of wind at my sleeve. Any bit of wind was refreshingly welcome. I closed my eyes with pleasure until I suddenly realized that a dust devil, a small cyclone, had come upon us from behind. For a few excited, panicked seconds, Gen and I were engulfed in sand, a whirlwind pulling at our clothing and filling our hair with grit.

After it passed, my teeth crunched on the abrasive particles. I tried to spit sand out of my mouth. Both of us stood and wiped sand from our skin, shook it out of our hair, and brushed it off our clothes. We laughed all the way to the truck. It wasn't until I climbed into the cab that I realized the wind had whirled off with my hat.

10 Mirage

I became intimidated by the landscape at Nata. The vastness of the desert, the long line of horizon, caused me to wrestle with indecision. Was my search for Freddy just tilting at windmills? Since I had no idea where he lived in this great expanse of desert, maybe it was time for me to adjust my goals. Looking at a map, I didn't even know where to start. Perhaps my new plan could be learning about the landscape and important places in the Kalahari, so that at least I wouldn't leave Botswana in complete ignorance.

I had plenty of time during our stay at Nata Lodge to adjust to this new way of thinking, but I came to the conclusion that this alternative plan would never give me a feeling of success. I still wanted to make contact with a San group. Above all, I wanted to meet Freddy Morris.

Two days after we arrived at Nata — two days of drinking salty tea with breakfast and hearing Livingstone's words hum through my mind, ". . . the only remedy is to get away as quickly as possible" — I checked our water and made sure that the built-in water tanks were full.

As we drove away from Nata, I had one last errand. I had to replace the hat lost on our visit to the pans. I lost hats all the time. But with the glare of the desert and the potential for sunburn, a hat was a necessity. Near the junction, I saw a shop in the back of a large sandy parking area. The sign said Groceries and Mercantile. I thought I might find a hat inside. Something practical, not too stylish.

As much as I might deny that self-image affects my taste in head-wear, the truth is I learned about symbolic associations with hats when I ran away from home. At age ten, I read too much, had a big imagination, and loved adventure. I saved money from my paper route and gathered my camping gear. During my spring vacation, while my parents were at work, I left the house and hitchhiked into the desert of Eastern Washington carrying a pack and wearing a coonskin cap, ready for the wilderness. I'd been gone for two days when I sat down in a small café and a blond waitress brought me a slice of homemade apple pie à la mode.

It may not have been coincidence that the sheriff of Kittitas County happened to sit down next to me in the restaurant. In fact, the waitress may have called him. She had seen my backpack and asked me why I was alone. She apparently didn't believe my story that I was earning a Boy Scout merit badge by surviving in the wilderness. After the sheriff came, she brought him a cup of coffee and pretty soon, he started to chat.

Nice man. The sheriff let me finish my pie before he arranged for free transportation back to Seattle.

When I returned home, the newspaper published a picture of me with my pack and coonskin. The publicity made me a celebrity in my own mind, and I wore the hat everywhere, until one day, I put the coonskin on my head and climbed into the back seat of the family's '37 Ford. I still remember my father's dark brow and angry eyes as he caught sight of me in the rearview mirror. He turned in the seat and scowled at me. "I don't want to see you wear that damn hat ever again."

In the Groceries and Mercantile store at Nata junction, three hats hung from the end of nearly bare shelves. The first hat was a broad-brimmed straw hat. Too big. It wouldn't even fit in the cab of the truck. The second was a knitted balaclava that rolled down to cover your face on a cold morning. Much too hot. The third was a baseball cap. It was Day-Glo lime, with a New York Yankees logo. It went well with my Seattle Mariners T-shirt. I tried it on. What would my father think if he could see me now? I bought the hat and got back into the truck.

We headed back onto the highway, and made the turn west on to the Nata-Maun road. It was one of the worst in Botswana. Driving the bumpy road, wash-boarded and rocky, through apparent nothingness, was a teeth-rattling experience.

Inside the cab, everything was vibrating, including our seat, and the vibrations made it too noisy for conversation.

The horizon was absolutely flat, a straight line with no break except for a few trees silhouetted along the road.

For hours, a pond seemed to shimmer across the road ahead. It was difficult to know for sure what I was seeing. Was it a lake? No, I knew it was a mirage, but it distorted the landscape. A mirage is an optical trick that makes one see a false image. But a mirage is partly in the mind, as I learned driving west on the Nata-Maun Road. Behind the wheel of the truck, I saw the horizon, miles ahead. It was a straight line in the distance, suggesting a sharp drop-off ahead. I was headed straight for it.

During that drive I was reminded of elementary school, when we learned about the perception of the world before Columbus made his voyage. We were shown a photograph of a mapmaker's drawing of a ship in mortal danger of spilling over a huge cataract. In the drawing, some ships were already going over the edge The doomed crew clung to masts, hair standing straight, mouths agape showing teeth and tongues. Others wore an expression I'd seen on faces of friends riding a roller coaster: open-eyed as the car approaches the top of an incline.

I also remembered a conversation I'd had shortly after arriving in Botswana. On that African morning, I was talking to a young Motswana science teacher as we walked side by side toward his school. He was from a nearby village and in his first term of teaching. He was dressed in a neatly pressed suit and wearing a newly purchased wristwatch. It was 6:30 a.m. and the sun shone pink in the eastern sky. We walked along a road where the droppings of sheep and goats littered the red sand and I told him I had talked on the phone the night before with friends in Seattle. I mentioned that my friends had just gotten out of bed and they were fixing breakfast when I called.

"How does it happen they were just waking up?" he asked. "You called them at night."

I told him about the time difference between Africa and the West Coast of the United States. The man looked at his brand-new wristwatch, and then back at me. Clearly, he was confused. Was I making a joke at his expense?

I touched my foot to the accelerator and drove into the undulating heat waves, and felt the momentum carry us west, like a current, taking us into the unknown. The horizon up ahead certainly looked like the edge of the world. In a sense, it really was. We were driving toward an unknown future that lay beyond that line. *What is waiting over the horizon? I don't know, and I won't know until we travel a few more days and let the future reveal its secret.*

After hours of the droning engine noise, jostling on the unpaved road, and driving directly into bright sunlight, my head felt thick. We'd driven well over a hundred miles from Nata and it was a relief to turn the key and shut off the engine. We had left the main road to make camp near a circle of ancient baobab trees at a place called Baines Baobabs. The spot was made famous in a nineteenth-century oil painting by explorer and painter, Thomas Baines. Reproductions of the image from his painting hang in dentists' offices all over southern Africa. The image is reproduced on postcards, in safari literature, and in airline magazines.

As soon as we were out of the truck, we left the bright glare of desert and walked into a grove of baobabs to make tea. The grove smelled damp and musty. A hundred yards away, a dry salt pan glistened in the blinding afternoon light.

Overhead, fuzzy pods of pear-sized fruit dangled from long stems. A recent rain had left the sandy soil slightly damp. Clumps of tall grass littered with last year's brown leaves surrounded the clearing where we chose to take our break.

At that moment I was too tired to think about where I was or what I was doing. I flipped two buckets upside down for stools and set up our single burner butane cooker to heat tea water. Gen pulled two semi-cold tins of beer from the cooler.

With a glazed stare, I watched the cooker. Roots of the large baobabs lay over the ground like misshapen fingers. Sitting under the branches of trees, I always feel an immediate sense of trust. It was easy for me to slip into a reverie that recurs from time to time, a daydream about sleeping in a forest with my father. It's a reassuring image I carry with me.

Behind us was the sloping twisted trunk of the giant tree. Water pooled in gaps left by branches fallen off long ago. Gen spread a napkin like a small tablecloth on top of a log and made a decorative arrangement of crackers and cheese.

We sat on our buckets without talking, quietly resting, rehydrating, and replenishing. We'd only been on our makeshift stools for five minutes when a skink with a long snake-like tail darted up a tree trunk. It was being chased by another skink. The second lizard was tailless, bitten off by a predator, perhaps.

Not a minute later, the two chased between my sprawled legs. They raced up another sloping trunk, followed closely by a thin gray snake, three feet in length, whipping over the damp earth near my feet, then up the deformed tree. The sight of the snake shook me out of my daze and reminded me to pay attention.

In Botswana, venom comes packaged in many different forms — as the diamond pattern on the spreading hood of a spitting cobra or curled innocuously as a napping puff adder. Rarely, it is encountered as the gray-scaled skin of a black mamba, notoriously attracted to moisture and small animals. And under any leaf or log, venomous scorpions lurk.

When we finished our tea and snack, Gen and I did not need a long discussion about where to set up our tent. We found a flat place in open ground, away from the trees.

Night in Africa. Darkness closes over the entire world like an eyelid, leaving a black sky. A deep-red glow lingers in the west. Stars become visible as the blood-red color fades. The Southern Cross, a kite-shaped constellation of four stars, twinkles faintly at first and then becomes more prominent as the sky darkens. Soon you see the rising shape of another constellation that appears to revolve around the Cross.

There was no moon when Gen and I stood at the edge of the pan looking up at the sky. The only light came from the Milky Way, and the starlight was bright enough to cast shadows on the ground behind us. I inhaled deeply, breathing in space and emptiness.

A noisy rustling of leaves and a rattle of twigs in the trees startled me. I could not see the cause and went to the tent where I groped blindly for my flashlight. The noise became louder by the time I got back to the pan's edge. With the beam of light I spotted a light-colored African barn owl perched on a branch. He fluttered his wings and shook the leaves. In the upper limbs another owl appeared. Within a few minutes, a group of four owls made the leaves chatter in the tree.

With an eerie wavering screech, one began circling the baobabs. Then the others left their perches to fly around the trees, screeching and howling, crashing through branches. They swooped through camp, batting the air with their huge wings. For an hour I followed them with the flashlight beam.

When I turned off the light, the owls became shadowy shapes. The great wheel of the sky revolved above. Under it, Gen and I connected by holding hands. We were inside the movement of an immense sphere that marked the time as surely as a ticking clock. Stars rotated around the Southern Cross, Orion's belt tipped to the west as we witnessed the constant motion of the universe.

The stars rotating in the sky made everything seem inevitable. I should have felt reassured. Yet I continued to sense uncertainty. Perhaps the forces that controlled life on this planet were different than the forces in the larger universe.

My thoughts about the unpredictability of life stirred a memory from my adolescence, the period of my life when I realized that the family I'd grown up with, was coming to an end. It began on the day my father walked across the living room and stumbled on a small rug. And then it happened again and again. Tripping and falling became a daily occurrence and soon after he received a medical diagnosis that gave him only a couple of years to live.

After his diagnosis, he moved to San Francisco to try to get some of his music published. In my rare moments of rationality as a fourteen year old, I understood that my father was a musician and wanted recognition before he died. But another meaning pushed its way into my adolescent brain — one I couldn't ignore. Perhaps he was delivering a message: This is only a temporary place and my commitment to you is only temporary.

When he died a year later, it left a huge gap in my life. Later, I tended to make friends with older co-workers, often asking them for advice, seeking compliments, or making conversation. But I knew it was unrealistic to try making a stranger a substitute for an irrevocable loss.

Standing there in the Kalahari Desert with Gen and gazing up at the stars at the edge of the pan, I felt how vulnerable we were to whatever the universe might want to throw our way. How vulnerable we were to loneliness and longing — and to loss.

I let myself feel the insecurity that comes from living in a universe ruled by chance. Reminded that life was always in flux, I felt the risk of change.

Uncertainty. Unpredictability. I had no job. Without a job, I had no place in the world.

When my father died, I went to work. In that moment of looking up at the sky, it struck me that being without a job was like being without a parent. Like a parent, my jobs had always structured my time and my life, and told me that I was worth something. Looking at the sky, I remembered part of a quote from Kierkegaard: ". . . he who is willing to work gives birth to his own father . . .." The philosopher explained why I felt so nervous about being unemployed. I'd clung to work all of my life. Without a job, I'd lost my surrogate father.

That morning, I'd seen the deceptive flatness of the earth. Now all I saw was sky. Confronted by the immensity, I felt insignificant and in need of another person to hold onto. At that moment, I could feel the predictability of flatness and the distortions of the universe and was aware of the coldness of space. But I also felt Gen's hand, the warmth of her skin and her softness. The feelings brought me back to earth, to a scale of things I could understand. We embraced.

The screeching of the owls continued into the early hours, long after we crawled into the tent to sleep.

11 Meeting the Trickster

Breakfast was leisurely. We sat near the tent away from the baobab grove. I could see the trees and the high branches where the owls had perched, but there was no sign of the large birds this morning.

At seven o'clock it was time to get ready to move on. That morning our objective was ten miles north to Nxai Pan — pronounced Nye Pan by non-native speakers. The "x" in the spelling of the name signifies a click sound, which most foreigners don't want to deal with.

As we walked to the truck, early morning shadows highlighted the tracks our tires had made in the sand the day before. But there was another groove not made by our tires. Imprinted in the loose sand was a twisting, reptilian trail that followed our tracks. A creature as fat as a small motorbike tire had left its imprint. Puff adder was my guess. Twenty feet from the back of the truck, I saw where the snake's trail notched the sand as it had turned to head into tall grass.

I was happy to leave this place and started the engine. We followed a narrow rutted road away from the baobabs. The fine sand pulled the truck from one side to the other and made the back wheels spin without traction. I jumped out of the truck and twisted the hubs on the two front wheels in order to engage the four-wheel drive. I had already performed the ritual several times. I would set the four-wheel drive and then the road would improve so I would reset the hubs, but ten minutes later we would find ourselves spinning and again in need of four-wheel drive.

There were three small *rondevaals* — small circular houses with conical roofs — clustered at the gate to Nxai Pan National Park. Nearby sat a square concrete-block building hardly bigger than a dumpster — the office. Inside, a slender man sat on a stool. I waited in the truck expecting him come out with something for me to sign. But after a minute it was clear he wasn't going to leave the shade. I got out and walked into the small office.

"You are from?" he asked.

I ran through a list of possible answers. I could tell him I'm from the USA or Seattle. But what he wanted to know was where we camped in order to arrive at nine-thirty that morning.

"We spent the night in the baobabs," I said.

"The baobabs are part of the park, you know." His tone seemed officious. "Campers on that side must pay 70 pula each for the night."

I was flabbergasted. "That's news to me. I didn't know." I argued with him. If the baobabs were part of Nxai Pan, it was a recent action. "It isn't posted," I said. "And if we'd simply driven back to the highway, you wouldn't have charged us."

I was beginning to puff up with self-righteous energy. "Look," I said. "One hundred forty pula to camp there is unreasonable. In the baobabs there have been no improvements." I paused to make sure he understood my English. "Besides, the night before last, we paid only five pula to camp at Nata Lodge."

My resistance made him nervous. He'd begun to tap and shuffle with his feet on the concrete. "Right," he said, "this one time I can overlook the camping fee. But you will pay 70 pula each for the nights you camp within the park."

I hadn't expected him to back down, but when I nodded and agreed to pay for camping, he relaxed immediately. Almost joyfully, he made a transformation from an officious bureaucrat into a gracious host. "My name is Richard," he said as he began filling out a registration form.

I heard the truck door click shut and saw Gen adjust the wide brim of her straw hat. She started toward the office. Apparently, she'd heard me arguing and thought something interesting might develop. "How much?" she asked as she entered.

"We're paying 140 pula a night."

"We've never had to pay, have we? For nearly three years. Shocking."

As expat teachers with a resident stamp in our passports, we'd paid the same fees as a citizen of Botswana. Never more than ten pula. Now that we were unemployed, we paid the full fare.

"We were hoping to see a lion," I said to Richard in order to change the subject.

"Yes, they live here. We have one pride living in the park and at least one solitary male, maybe more." Richard began to sound chatty. "Lions cause us many problems." He pointed over to one of the rondevaals about thirty feet from the office. "I sleep there. When others are on duty, they do too. Aii! Let me tell you . . . none of us sleep easy. It's very hot, but we have to sleep with doors closed." His speech was punctuated by high-pitched whoops. "Aii, lions will enter if a door is open."

His desk was the size of a tray. As he talked, he printed information from our passports onto the registration forms. "The park ranger kills a steenbok for meat to feed the workers once a week," he said. "Lions hear the smell and come into our compound."

I did a double take. It took me a moment before I realized "hear" was probably a good description. Lions were attracted to meat in pursuit of a meal. Maybe they do hear the smell of meat. For all I know, it's an experience that uses all their senses.

He charged us in advance for three nights and gave us a copy of the form. I turned to leave. I had the yellow copy in my hand and was starting to fold the sheet in half when Richard said, "It is not safe to sleep out in the open."

Of course we were planning to sleep in the open — we'd just paid him for three nights of camping. Walking back to the truck, Gen and I looked at each other, suppressing a laugh.

"Maybe we should have only paid for one night," I said.

"I was thinking the same thing," she replied. "If we're attacked the first night, how do we get our money back?"

Gen was more fascinated by the wildlife in Africa than she was afraid. We had camped many times in Botswana or Zimbabwe when animals had entered our camp during the night. Once, our tent was rocked by a careless grazing hippo. It jarred the tent and I sat up immediately to see what was happening. She slept through it.

On another occasion, I was awakened by the roar of a distant lion and the screeching laughter of hyenas. Gen woke up, too, and began making preparations to use the potty bucket outside the tent. "There are hyenas in the vicinity. Don't go out," I said.

But she was determined. "I have to go pee, whether there are hyenas or not." Despite my warning, she went out. The next morning we found hyena tracks throughout the camp.

As we left the office, Richard gave us a map. It showed that the park was almost a square, roughly twenty-five miles on each side. Snaking through the park were more than one hundred miles of road. In order to get oriented, I drove the unpaved loop that meandered through the park while Gen held the map. When we came to a T, she said, "Up here, turn right."

Driving past low scrub trees we entered alkaline grassland dotted with acacia shrubs and termite mounds. Nxai Pan was dry and flat. No one I have asked has ever been able to tell me which San group gave Nxai Pan its name or what the word means, but it must have been a prime site for San hunters at one time. There is a lot of wildlife and the flat terrain makes for excellent visibility. It would be easy to believe that hundreds of generations hunted here.

I drove slowly, our windows open. Groves of tall trees rose like islands a hundred yards from the road. Mixed herds of giraffe, zebra, and antelope grazed in the shade.

"I'd like a better look," Gen said.

I stopped the truck and we took turns gazing at the animals through binoculars. Our presence made some of the animals visibly nervous. The zebras formed a defensive half-circle and appeared ready for action before we drove on.

We stayed on the main loop, stopping frequently to look through binoculars or take pictures. Stacks of bones lay in the sand near the road. They were not in random piles, but seemed to have been arranged by park employees. Rib cages, skulls, and leg bones whitened in the bright sun. I remember Richard's warning about lions.

David Livingstone may have been referring to Nxai Pan when he wrote about passing ". . . quickly over a hard country, which is perfectly flat. A little soil lying on calcareous tufa, over a tract of several hundreds of miles, supports a vegetation of fine sweet short grass, and mopane and baobab trees."

The tall trees Gen and I saw were mostly camel thorn. The pods scattered on the ground below the trees provided a rich source of protein for grazing animals. Giraffes nibbled at the branches, gathering the pods right at their source.

On one side of the zigzagging road, we came upon dozens of uprooted mophane trees. They lay on the ground, stripped of leaves.

"Look at this. Curious."

"Why are these trees here?" Gen asked. "The soil on the roots is fresh."

Then we saw heaps of elephant dung. "A band of bachelor males must have come this way."

Our loop passed around an area identified on the map as Khama Khama Pans. In the northern part of the loop, a few mud holes gave evidence of a localized rain. Despite the rain a few days before, the ground had a caked and cracked appearance. In the distance, a body of water shimmered. A grove of trees was reflected perfectly. I drove closer to get a photograph, but it was a mirage.

Steenbok were everywhere. The small dry-area antelopes are the size of Great Danes and able to survive for years only on the moisture they get from plants. The back leg of the antelopes always appears under tension, like a coiled spring. Every time we stopped the truck near a steenbok, it gave us a look of astonishment, ready to leap.

Near a turn in the road, a pair of large birds ran ahead of us along the main tire tracks. Kori bustards, standing nearly five feet tall. I stopped and the birds slowed their pace to a walk. Then I let the truck roll forward and gradually we caught up to them. At the point where we could see the straight white-feathered crown that gave them their cartoonish look, they began to run again. Then, reluctantly, they took to the air, settling a hundred yards away. Eventually, they moved to one side of the road to let us pass. The minute we'd gone by, they returned to the convenience of tire tracks.

I was fascinated watching the wildlife. Humans have a connection with animals that's hard to explain. In our rational/scientific culture, scientists can point to our shared DNA. The San have noticed the connection, as well, but have a different kind of explanation. According to their stories, in the earliest times, people and animals lived together in one village. That was before they all became distinct creatures. For the San, observing animals was like watching neighbors go through their daily routines in their own unique manner.

Here in Nxai Pan, Gen and I were observing all of the inhabitants of that original village, with the exception of the San.

A group of gemsbok grazed casually in nonchalant groups of a dozen or so. They barely noticed our presence. The calm attitude of these large antelopes was a contrast with the zebras, probably due to the fact that they are equipped with long razor-sharp antlers and are well able to defend themselves against predators. They had long tails and carried themselves like well-bred horses. The black-and-white markings around their eyes reminded me of the medicine marks on a warrior's painted face. Some San groups hold special healing ceremonies in which men apply black and white marks to their faces and the shaman carries a wand of coarse hair from a gemsbok's tail.

Rounding a turn in the road, I became distracted by the antics of another pair of kori bustards running ahead of us. I didn't want to make the birds nervous and so I applied the brakes. At that moment, we passed a cluster of trees and close to the driver's side door, a pair of jackals trotted through short grass next to the road.

Their fur was the color of faded cinnamon with a black saddle on the back. At first, they seemed as surprised as we were, but they stood their ground. The tables had been turned. All morning, we had been the viewers. Animals had reacted to us studying them. Now, these two watched us with a cunning expression that I knew couldn't last. They would be curious for a few seconds, and then turn and run.

But they didn't. Instead, they sat in the sand. I still expected them to dash off, but these two had an attitude. For a minute, they stared boldly, with aggressive, scolding expressions. *We're in charge here. Did you register at the gate? Do you have your receipt?* The female seemed put out by our presence. She was a haughty hostess and we had dropped in at an inconvenient time, uninvited and unexpected. Such impudence. She scratched her ear as she scooted around in the sand, turning her back on us.

The male was the first to stand. He shook himself, and then began to romp in a circle like someone's pet dog. *Let's have a chase. You make the first move.*

That's when I recognized him as the trickster, acting his part.

There's a reason the jackal is the hero of many San stories, portrayed as a character not brave or confrontational, but one who wins through cleverness. The jackal is the type of hero who wins by trickery, lies, and narrow escapes.

The trickster is the shape-shifter whose identity is always ambiguous. Is the jackal a wild animal or a domestic dog? His apparent sense of humor implies a sympathy bond with humans. But beware! The trickster means trouble. The trickster takes many forms: mantis, snake, even a man can become inhabited by the trickster spirit. When he's in the vicinity, malicious accidents are apt to happen.

The female seemed to grow tired of the game as we watched the male's antics. She'd waited patiently. Finally, she stood, gave her tail a haughty shake, and began to walk off. The male's attention had been on me, the man in the truck. However, when the female made her move, the male became indecisive. After a moment's hesitation, with a brief look over his shoulder, he turned and joined her. The two trotted off through the grass, and then disappeared into a clump of bushes.

Three days passed and we did not see another human being. The faces of animals took on more personality. The jackal-trickster was never far from my thoughts.

Night after night, a barn owl flew screeching above us for fifteen minutes. But he was well-behaved compared to the owls at Baines Baobabs. Each night, as we lay in our tent before going to sleep, we heard the calls of jackals in the night, the howl and the descending yips that mimic the coyote of North America. Gen and I tried to scare each other with stories about lions. My tales never worked. Gen is fearless.

Around our camp each night, wildlife was curiously missing. We had a few spring hares hop through the neighborhood and a great many birds. But no lions and no snakes.

Friday morning we cleaned up around camp in preparation for the drive into Maun. A pair of yellow hornbills poked through the ashes of our fire as we packed up. Above us, a lilac-breasted bird sang in the limbs of a tree. The day was warm and both of us wore shorts and sandals. Gen put away kitchen supplies while I took down the tent, rolled it up, and set it to one side. We were nearly packed, but I needed help folding the plastic ground cloth, a piece of black plastic folded double.

It needed shaking out and so each of us grabbed an end and shook vigorously. Then I carried the tent to the truck and Gen went to work on the now grit-free ground cloth, meticulously folding it as it lay on the sandy soil.

Tucking the tent behind the water can, I stopped what I was doing when I heard Gen's scream.

Gen cried out, "I've been bitten!" When I got to her, she was sitting on a campstool with her bare foot outstretched. Her sandal lay on the ground.

"Scorpion!" she said. "I think it came out of the ground cloth."

The black plastic was still on the ground and beside it a scorpion, light brown, an inch and a half in length, had met his demise in the sand.

"You're lucky," I said. "It's the least dangerous kind." We'd had to contend with larger scorpions in the past. They were black with a big round sac of venom. Gen took very little comfort from my assurances. She said it felt like a flame from a blowtorch near the big toe, though I could see no swelling yet.

"Do we have any information on scorpion bites?" she asked.

I looked for our first-aid manual in the truck. The book covered first-aid possibilities in Latin America and Africa. I read aloud from the section on scorpion bites.

"Some scorpion bites may be worse than others . . . ."

Gen's foot was on fire. She wrinkled her nose disdainfully.

"Emetine injected around the sting greatly reduces pain." I added sarcastically, "I'll get the syringe out of the refrigerator." Of course, we had no way of administering an injection.

" *'Put ice on the sting.'* Hah! Is the ice cube tray in the freezer?" I laughed. "Helpful advice in a national park in Africa. The nearest ice is a hundred miles away." Gen raised her palm and waved my words away with an impatient gesture.

"Aspirin! We have that. In the glove compartment." I grabbed the container and handed it to her. A bottle of water was just behind her in the truck.

"To adults, scorpion stings are rarely dangerous." I repeated the phrase to reassure Gen, and told her I didn't think it would be any worse than a bad bee sting.

"What do they know?" She sounded angry.

"Let's go back to the gate," I said. "I'm sure Richard has had experience with scorpions." Also, I thought Gen might appreciate local advice. She massaged her aching foot in the truck while I threw the few remaining belongings in the back and we headed off.

Richard was in the office.

"What do you do for scorpion bites?"

"Aii, we get stung all the time," Richard said, and then laughed. "Aspirin and mud."

Gen had taken a couple of aspirin by that time. We found a tire track near the office where mud had caked, and by mixing a little water into it, we had enough to make a mud plaster that covered her entire foot.

We bounced our way through the sand back to the highway and kept adding water when the mud on her foot began to dry. I wondered how she felt, but I didn't ask. For long stretches during our drive, Gen closed her eyes and tried to rest. In places, the road was so bad it took my complete attention to navigate the ruts and avoid the jarring from deep holes. Despite the mud poultice and the aspirin, the inferno in her foot lasted two more hours.

I felt terrible. *I should have been the one who rolled up the ground cloth so that it was me who was bitten, not her. I should have been able to do more to quell the fire in her foot.*

Driving west for miles and miles, I had to slow the truck almost to a crawl because of road construction. A Japanese company was building a paved highway that would replace the one we were on. As I navigated around detours and earth movers, my thoughts drifted back to the jackals in Nxai Pan. What I had seen showed me that they were intelligent creatures with a sense of humor. I felt fond feelings toward them, similar to how I felt with friendly dogs. But I knew that jackals had a reputation for dishonesty, cunning, and even criminal behavior. Had I been gulled by these tricksters?

The truck crawled along at a snail's pace, and before long I was daydreaming again about riding in my father's Ford on the day he left for San Francisco. It had seemed like there was a real possibility that I might never see him again and I'd felt the presence of a trickster in my life. Until shortly before that day, my life had been stable and the family around me seemed permanent — and then it wasn't. It was as though my world was suddenly tossed into the air and all the pieces scattered. I was being taught the lessons of impermanence, but it felt like a cruel joke.

It was late Friday afternoon when we entered the town of Maun. Gen's foot had finally cooled down, and at the edge of town we stopped to sweep the caked mud from the floor of the truck and to clean her foot.

On the outskirts of Maun, road-building equipment sat parked behind chain-link fences. Construction was underway all over town. The main roads in Maun were newly paved and smelled like fresh tar. Everywhere, white sand drifted across the black asphalt.

We both needed a cool drink and so I drove directly to Reilly's Hotel. It was a place with a colorful history. At one time, Reilly's had been a gathering place for hunters, desert adventurers, and safari operators. Now it was just a stopover for businessmen and government officials on their way to Ghanzi. The decor had all the personality of a Ramada Inn.

Tables under umbrellas were arranged around the lawn. We took a seat and a waiter brought two cans of warm cola and glasses filled with ice. The ice melted as soon as I poured the drinks.

As I settled into my chair, I realized I was slipping into a funk. The sight of the paved roads and the remodeled hotel disturbed me. Maybe I was longing for something that had been lost. Part of my low mood had to do with my awareness that in the Kalahari, any signs of progress, made the area more inhospitable for San culture.

Gen was quiet as well. There was a look in her eye that I recognized. She was a long way away. We sipped our drinks in silence.

We intended to fill the gas tank, buy groceries, and depart Maun as soon as we'd taken care of our thirst. Leaving Reilly's, we drove into the business district. To our surprise and dismay, everything was closed. The one grocery store in town was locked and the sign on the door listed hours of business: Monday through Friday. Employees at the gas station had gone home for the weekend. We hadn't planned on spending the weekend in Maun, but it didn't look as if we had a choice.

We found a place to stay at the Crocodile Camp on the edge of town, but before long I began to think of it as a "good news-bad news" joke. The place had plenty of space available. In fact, we were the only guests. The camping area was deep with white sand. A tall thorn tree in one corner provided the only shade. We were surrounded by a tattered reed fence. The camp was not exactly a visitor's paradise. During tourist season, safari trucks used the camp as a one- or two-night stopover for clients, and the drivers took the opportunity to repair their trucks. Piles of greasy spare parts had been deposited next to the fence at one end of the campground.

We pitched our tent under the tree. The outdoor toilet-shower-laundry area — a long building with a line of sinks and broken mirrors — faced the campground. Almost immediately, I discovered that the water had been shut off in the toilet. I needed to find the manager. At the foot of a sloping walk near a swimming pool, I found her. A blond woman surrounded by a group of friends. A man splashed in the pool. The others sat at a round table overlooking the nearly dry river channel of the *Thamalakalane*, or Crocodile River.

I described the problem with the water, and she answered my questions in a voice tinged with a British accent. Then she called out in German to the man in the swimming pool. He climbed dripping out of the pool, grabbed a pipe wrench, and walked with me up to the camp to turn on the water.

Even with the water turned on, the camp felt desolate. Neither of us wanted to spend the evening there. Fortunately, we had been to Maun once before and remembered a small restaurant called the Duck Inn near the airport. We drove there, and a waitress led us to a table in a room separated from the main dining area. We ordered Chicken Kiev, and I asked the waitress to bring us two cartons of peach juice while we waited for our food.

Music blared from a speaker on a shelf directly across the small room. The volume was turned up so high neither of us recognized the lyrics at first. Finally, I realized it was Frank Sinatra singing, "Luck be a lady tonight . . .." Only after we sat a minute, did the words begin to make sense. "I'm the guy that you came in with . . .." It was deafening.

There were no windows in the room where we sat, but on the wall opposite our table was a framed collage of photographs. The photos all showed a bearded, sunburned European man in the desert, drinking a beer or driving a dune buggy. The largest photo was a close-up, the man's head wrapped in a towel like a turban. Something about the way the pictures were displayed gave me the impression I was looking at a shrine.

Our waitress was a frail-looking, dark-skinned woman. I asked her about the photographs. She looked at the collage on the wall as if she were seeing it for the first time. "No," she said after a few seconds of examination, "I don't know that man."

After a few minutes, a tall blond woman swooped into the room, a drink in her hand. She was probably about forty-five and she wore skintight black-and-white slacks and a black T-shirt with "Duck Inn" in gold letters emblazoned across the front. "Is that music too loud?" she asked pointing to the speaker.

Setting her drink on an empty table, she hopped up on a chair and disconnected a wire. The volume dropped immediately, although we could still hear the music from a speaker in the adjoining room.

The woman pulled a bar stool close to our table and sat down. "In town for a while, are you?"

"We're at Croc Camp until Monday," I said. "Can't leave before we get groceries and petrol."

"Yeah, everything closes in this town until eight o'clock Monday morning." Her voice sounded breezier than either Gen or I felt about the delay.

Gen asked, "Is this your restaurant?"

The woman bounced up to grab her drink and brought it over to the table. "Yes, my business," she said with obvious pride. I tried to place her accent.

She took a sip of her drink through a straw and said, "I'm from Switzerland, but I came here from Nairobi fourteen years ago. There was a trend for hunters and safari people to move from Nairobi to Maun and I was part of that."

She leaned back on her stool and gazed into space. "In those days I was with a hunter. You'd think it would be a romantic way of life, but I got very bored. The man was always in the bush. So, I asked myself, what can I do with my spare time? By fits and starts, I opened this place. It was probably 1980 before the business really got going."

"You've seen Maun change a lot," I said.

"Change? Nothing stays the same for long, but here it's drastic. The population is now twenty-eight thousand and we're having a boom. I don't trust booms because they're always going to end. The end of a boom will be a crash and you can see it coming. Everyone's acting as if there's no end in sight." Her voice maintained its breezy manner, even as she talked about potential calamity.

Reaching for her glass, she took another sip. "But I feel cautious," she said. "There really isn't much money in this town. Some people joke that there is only about 10,000 pula in Maun and it keeps getting passed around from one business to another."

I asked about the pictures on the wall.

Her expression became serious as she swept a bit of blond hair away from the side of her face. "He was a friend. Very well known." Her tone became tender. "Jack Bowsfield was his name. Ever hear of him?"

I hadn't.

"I knew him in Nairobi. Met him again when I came here." She paused to clear her throat. Then began again, "Jack used to live in the desert. He operated a resort and took people out on dune buggy safaris on the pans. He did some funny things, too. He'd land his plane on the field across the street from here." Her eyes began to tear up.

"Often, after he landed, he'd forget to tie the plane down. But we get these strong winds here. The winds are strong enough to turn over an airplane." She laughed, "And he found it that way. Jack's plane was upside down next to the hangar." She spoke as if she were sharing a funny experience that happened yesterday.

As the waitress placed our dinner on the table, the woman stood. "Nice talking to you," she said. With business-like strides, she disappeared around the corner.

I began to cut into my chicken and heard the music over the speaker in the next room. "Regrets, I've had a few . . .," same Sinatra CD, ". . . and more than this, I did it my way."

Later, the owner came past the table and saw we'd finished our peach drinks. She brought two more cartons. "On the house," she said.

Like most everyone, we had no reason to be in Maun except to wait. Maun is a crossroads, a safari jumping off place, a supply center, an airport — a town that people come to in order to get to someplace else.

A storm passed through that night as Gen and I slept in our tent. I was awakened by an angry crash of thunder and flashes of lightning. It was raining hard. Our tent was soaked, though we managed to keep our bedding dry.

In the morning, wet sand clung to the soles of our sandals and made them heavy on our feet. Rain had been falling all the previous week in Maun, so the firewood I purchased was soaked. I struggled to get a fire going in order to make tea and breakfast. Both of us gathered twigs, and I put a piece of candle into our steaming pile of sticks. Once the candle managed to dry the twigs, the kindling flamed up and the mophane logs began to burn.

Finally I could boil water in our enameled metal pot over the open fire. I did everything in the usual way, except that when I took the pan off the fire, the handle was hotter than I expected. Acting quickly, I grabbed a striped cloth to use as a hot pad and set the pan on a rock.

"You're using our tea towel!" Gen yelled.

"There's no hot pad. The handle got too hot."

"That's what we use for drying dishes. You'll get soot on the towel."

I was burning my fingers and she was worried about a dish rag.

Later that morning, a Tswana man, wearing the blue tattered overalls workmen wear in Botswana, worked around the campground emptying garbage barrels. As he walked along the reed fence, I waved and asked, *"A re a bona pula, gompieno?"*

I intended the question as, "Are we going to have rain today?" But asking a question in future tense was beyond my language competence and what I actually said was, "Are we having rain today?"

The man looked up from his work. I could tell that he didn't quite know what to make of my question. It was not raining at the moment. He looked up at the sky and the parting clouds and smelled the warm air, undoubtedly wondering what I had meant. *"Ga ile,"* he said, a slightly bemused expression on his face. "It's not going to."

He knew what he was talking about. Late in the day, I heard a drum roll of thunder. Wind picked up and I smelled rain, but the clouds soon parted, the sky became brighter, the air warmed, and the afternoon became hot and muggy.

Throughout the weekend, Gen grew more and more distant. I attributed her remoteness to boredom and the irritation of being in a place without a purpose.

On Sunday, after going through the ritual of making a fire with wet wood, I made our tea. I threw a heaping tablespoon of leaves from our box of Five Roses into the boiling water and clamped the lid before removing the pan from the fire. I placed it on a flat stone, but the water continued to boil in the black pot.

After a few minutes, I removed the lid, added milk and sugar, and poured the tea into our cups. In a minute it was cool enough to sip.

"This tea is bitter. Way too strong!" Gen exclaimed.

"What's bothering you?" I asked. "The tea is the same as yesterday."

"Yesterday the tea was too strong. I didn't say anything."

A long silence followed.

"There is something," she said, finally. "This whole weekend I've been bothered. It's nothing. Really silly."

"Can't you tell me?"

"I don't know," she said. "I feel embarrassed. It's so silly."

"Something I'm doing?"

"Nothing you're doing."

"But something."

"I'm afraid it will come out wrong. I don't quite know how to put it into words . . .."

I sat quietly.

Finally, Gen said, "When I was bitten by the scorpion. I felt as if you were making fun."

"When I read out of the book?"

"Um hmm."

"You asked me to read from the first-aid book."

"Then you laughed the whole time."

"The recommendations seemed so useless."

"All the same, I was in pain. That bite scared me."

I nodded. I tried to apologize, but my words hung in the air between us.

"That's really the main thing. I was scared. I didn't know what a scorpion bite could do. And to you it was a joke. You told me it would be like a bad bee sting. What do you know anyway? It's my foot."

She was right.

"It's still there," Gen said after a long pause. "My toe has been tingling all weekend. Last night, I dreamed my foot turned black and my toes dropped off. I can't get it out of my mind."

A silence descended on us after that and we spent the morning in separate places. Gen disappeared with her sketchpad. For an hour or so, I read and made notes on yellow-lined pages in my notebook and watched as wind swirled gray, fine sand into small cyclones across the camp. As I watched I remembered that, in the stories of the San, those small whirlwinds were spirits come back from the dead to cause mischief for the living.

I had too much time to think. I thought about how we were getting closer to the town of Ghanzi, a government outpost that was still a day's drive to the west, but I didn't know any more about the old man named Freddy than when we started, and I doubted we'd ever find him. I thought about my poor grammar in Setswana. I wondered how it would feel to land an airplane at the Maun airport and the next morning find it upside down. For some reason, I kept seeing the face of a shape-shifting jackal. And I remembered how just a few days earlier I'd felt a sense of awe seeing the expanse of endless sky and desert. Now, by some fluke or bad joke, I was sitting alone in Maun staring at a reed fence and a pile of oily truck parts.

Until 8:00 a.m. on Monday morning, I was helpless. All I could do was to wait.

12 Into Unknown Territory

Monday morning we were able to buy groceries and put fuel into the tank. Clouds pressed low in the dark sky as we set out for Ghanzi. Rain still threatened two hours later when we stopped at a grocery in Toteng for a cold drink. Three hitchhikers sat leaning against their backpacks outside the store. I knew they were waiting for a ride and I was sure they saw me, but either because of shyness or my white skin, they said nothing. All three wore dreadlocks and one had a black T-shirt with a Day-Glo graphic of a Seattle rock band. The word Nirvana oozed across his chest like melted wax.

It was obvious to me that the men would get soaked if they stayed, so I greeted them in Setswana and asked where they were headed. After a long pause, one of the men plucked up enough nerve to answer, "Ghanzi." I invited them to ride with us, and two of the men climbed into the back of our truck with their packs, while the other, Lucas, who was the most fluent in English, climbed into the cab with Gen and me. After we had driven about fifty miles west Lucas told me they wanted to get out at a place called Dkar.

"Dkar?" I asked. "You said you were going to Ghanzi." Dkar was just a dot on the map on the way to Ghanzi. It was all the same to me, but I thought it was curious that they hadn't said that earlier.

Lucas wore sunglasses even on that cloudy day. The frame rode low on his nose and he peered at me over gold rims. "I did not think you know Dkar."

He was right; I didn't know the place. It wasn't on my radar at all. Anyway, my attention was focused elsewhere. We were driving over the worst road I had ever seen. A protrusion of granite or limestone — a remnant of some past geological event — chewed at our tires. I wondered what kind of trip the two hitchhikers in the back of the truck were having, but mostly I worried about the condition of our spare tire. At this rate, there was a strong possibility we would have to use it.

Where I dropped off the hitchhikers made no difference to me, I was determined to continue on to Ghanzi. I had a mental picture of Gen and me spending the night tented on a cool lawn behind the Kalahari Arms Hotel. But I asked anyway, "What's in Dkar?"

"You hear about the Basarwa? Bushmen?" Lucas said as he shook his dreadlocks. "Some people tell the Bushmen they're stupid. But in Dkar, no! 'You are smart. Regular people.' A very good place." He sounded like a one-man chamber of commerce. "Teachers there for the Bushmen. Teach Nharo to speak English, even. Write. Paint pictures and make crafts. You will like seeing the things Bushmen make. You should stay in Dkar."

He'd said Nharo. Dkar must be a Nharo village. That was interesting. Still, I had no intention of staying in Dkar, but I asked anyway. "Is there a place to pitch a tent?"

"In Dkar there is a hostel. You don't need a tent."

I looked across at Gen. The rough road was wearing on us both and neither of us said a word. She must have made a slight movement of her eyebrow. Whatever it was, it was all the communication we needed. *Why not?*

My mind began preparing for the unknown. I could visualize my tent on a patch of grass behind a hotel in Ghanzi, even if I had never seen the place, but I had no way of imagining what I'd find in Dkar.

Midday we crossed a divide where we found ourselves looking down from the height of Mabele-wa-pudi Hill — the Goat's Breast — at a brown plain below. A sharp line above us split the sky, dark and cloudy on one side, blue on the other. We were entering the Ghanzi district. Heading west toward that clear sky, the air suddenly became warmer.

Finally we arrived in Dkar, and what was unimaginable earlier in the day, became reality. I turned the key to shut down the engine, stepped down from the truck, and stood looking at Dkar, a place dustier and more desolate than Maun. Although my arms still tingled from the vibration of the steering wheel and I was relieved not to be driving any farther, I couldn't help but wonder why we'd decided to stay here even for a night.

Nothing was moderate about the place. It was three o'clock in the afternoon in February: the hottest time of the day in the hottest time of the year. The earth was sandy and the shrubs were thorny. Everything to the extreme.

We had parked in front of a crafts store painted in zebra stripes. I saw other concrete block buildings with corrugated metal roofs. Across the road, a Botswana TeleComs microwave tower rose into the air. A windmill perched atop a slight rise was supposed to turn in the wind to pump water. But there was no wind, only a man in blue coveralls leaning against a wooden rail fence in the windmill's shade.

The road that ran through the village was two sandy ruts, and the main highway into the western Kalahari. It continued west toward Ghanzi, twenty-five miles away. At the moment, there was no traffic coming or going.

I had a fleeting fantasy of escape to Ghanzi, and, for a moment, I was torn. But the decision had been made and I was not going to get back behind the wheel. As far as my body was concerned, the road stopped here — at least for the day.

Nothing moved. A shimmer of heat created a small mirage over the road. West of the village, where a cluster of thorn trees met the highway, a small dust devil began to twist. Beginning as a small stirring of sand and dry leaves, it levitated above the road, and then seemed to touch the earth for a few seconds, before lifting off as a column of dust and leaves. It meandered in my direction, and then hesitated to suck more sand into its eddy. A minute earlier the air had been still; now, a tug of wind whipped at my trousers.

I'd learned to become suspicious of these eddies of wind, these whirlwinds, ghosts of those who were never buried or properly mourned. Spirits that never rest and haunt the living as twisters.

It occurred to me that this restless spirit might be trying to steal my new hat or cause some other mischief, but then it took a sharp turn, twisting behind the building that housed the store. Sand pelted the concrete wall, making a pt-pt-pt, before the wind died and the air became still again.

The whirlwind was gone, vanished like the hitchhikers. I had helped them unload their packs from the back of the truck, and then closed the canopy and turned to say goodbye. But in the moment my back was turned, all three had disappeared.

Had there really been three hitchhikers, or had I dreamed them?

Gen stood on the other side of the truck. I saw her adjust the wide brim of her hat to an angle that gave her maximum shade, and then she crossed her arms and leaned on the fender, a wry expression on her face. We looked at each other across the glare of the truck's white hood. It was one of those silent glances that substitutes for conversation when we're too tired to do anything else.

What now?

A voice spoke to me from a primal center in my brain, Get a room! I obeyed. For the next several minutes I devoted every ounce of energy and concentration I had left to that task. I entered the zebra-striped store where a sign said Kuru Centre. Inside, the place had a few groceries, Bushman handicrafts, T-shirts, and souvenirs. Apparently it was also the place where dormitory arrangements were made. A blond woman in the store slid a guest register across the counter for me to sign. She pointed out the hostel building a few hundred yards away.

The hostel struck me as an unusual style of construction for this part of the world. It was a low wooden structure on a concrete pad with varnished logs notched at the corners. Blinding sunlight reflected off the metal roof.

I drove the truck alongside the narrow building and parked in what little shade it offered. When I got out of the truck, I could see the windmill and the same man in blue coveralls I'd seen earlier. There was no neighborly wave or other indication that he saw me. He bent to scoop a pail of water from a trough.

Our home for the night smelled like mosquito repellant. Ten metal cots lined the wall. Because Gen and I were the only guests, I pushed a couple of the cots under its one long window and moved the others out of the way. The metal legs howled as they scraped across the waxed concrete floor.

I carried sleeping bags and mosquito netting from the truck. Thorns attached themselves to the soles of my sandals and set me skating across the waxed surface. Inside the room, the polyurethane-treated logs and the polished floor glistened with reflected sunlight. The brightness was disorienting.

After moving our belongings into the room, I decided to walk the path through low scrub thorns from the hostel to the road. A few people had ventured out as the sun went lower in the sky, and I did my best to strike up conversations. Unfortunately, the only subject I was capable of talking about was the weather.

On the dusty road, near the place where I let out the hitchhikers, I met a man in a brown cotton coat. The man was small in stature and olive-skinned. He had the facial features of a Kalahari Bushman. His eyes were shaded by a floppy hat.

I greeted him in Setswana in the standard formal manner since I was a stranger. "*Dumela. O tsogile jang.*" Hello. How did you rise?

As soon as the words were out of my mouth, I realized the absurdity of the greeting on a hot afternoon.

"The day is very hot," I said in Setswana.

"*Thata!*" He agreed. Very hot.

"*Ga gona pula,*" I said, stating the obvious. There is no rain.

"There is no rain," he agreed.

A little further on, I greeted a woman walking out of a building. The conversation was the same with the same result. We exhausted conversational possibilities, and then she turned and walked on.

Confronted with the inadequacy of my language skills, I felt even more like an outsider. Why would anybody want to talk to a strange white man who speaks like a child?

I headed back through low acacia shrubs on a trail toward the hostel. Every few steps I had to stop to empty my sandals of sand and pick thorns out of my toes.

Fifty yards from my parked truck, I paused in the shadow of an A-frame building, the Dutch Reformed Church, according to a plaque near the door. I needed a moment to sort things out. How had I gotten into this impasse? I had wanted to learn more about the San and experience their culture. For some reason I thought locating an old man named Freddy Morris would help me accomplish that goal, and I convinced Gen it would be a good use of our time. Now, I found myself in this desert village.

After a few minutes of frustration, I did come to one conclusion: This was a Nharo village I was in. The people I met on the road were definitely Nharo Bushmen and Lucas had used the word Nharo. He and his friends must have been Nharo, but how could I have missed recognizing that?

Brilliant! Well, here I am. Now what?

So far, I hadn't had much luck striking up a conversation. If only I knew Nharo . . ., I thought. Then I remembered the language barrier I'd experienced in the Tsodilo Hills. I had driven away from there feeling discouraged and disillusioned. Had I driven all this way to re-learn the same lesson?

Returning to the hostel room, I found Gen busying herself, organizing belongings in boxes.

I pulled a bucket from the back of the truck and sat on it under an overhang in the doorway. The shade felt welcome. Between the hostel and church, a flock of goats nibbled with furious energy among low thorn shrubs. Anything green poking above the coarse red sand became part of their moving buffet. There wasn't much, and the goats had to cover a lot of ground.

I tried to clear my mind by watching the goats. I felt overwhelmed. Lucas had said that there were positive things going on in Dkar for the Bushmen. Maybe so, but at the moment all I could see was emptiness.

Gen wanted to cook on something besides the one-burner butane flame we had used for the last ten days. "There must be a kitchen here somewhere. I'm going to find it," she said. Wearing a pink blouse and denim culottes, she disappeared around the corner of the building.

Earlier, in the process of unloading the truck, I had piled some things on top of my cot. I now went back into the hostel and grabbed my notebook from the pile, I would go over the notes I'd scribbled at the library in Gaborone and during our travels.

Settling on the bucket, I leaned back against the wall just outside the doorway and tried to focus on the disorganized pages, but my mind wasn't really up to the task. Everything roared and bounced before my eyes, as if I were still driving a truck down a rough desert road.

I'd been an outsider for most of my time in Botswana and had gone through a series of arrivals in unfamiliar places. This trip had started on the other side of the country in Gaborone. From where I was sitting at that moment, Gaborone seemed like another world. We had camped at points across the desert: Nata, Makgadikgadi Pans, Baines Baobabs, Nxai Pan, Maun. Sitting on my bucket, I stared at a page and let the pictures from these experiences rush through my mind.

I was lost in thought when out of the corner of my eye something caught my attention. An insect clung to the wooden frame of the doorway just above the lower hinge. It was huge, half a foot long, and brilliant green.

Although he looked to be perfectly still, his antennae waved, and his triangular head, which seemed too small for the long body, rotated. Very slowly he eased himself up the frame. I could barely detect his movement. He moved stiffly, like a priest in a green frock.

I was close enough to see the parts of the segmented body — head, thorax, abdomen. Six legs. Antennae. The forelegs clasped in prayer. His green color on the brown doorframe seemed incongruous. The color made him stand out, but he moved with stealth. *How the hell did he get here? And why he is here?*

I had been told by Africans that if a creature comes into your space, pay attention. Wild creatures have their place. If they cross the boundary into a human's territory, it means something.

I remembered a time when an owl came into my office at the college. I had left a louvered window open, and when I came to work in the morning there was the bird, a foot-and-a-half tall, perched on a coat rack. "An owl in your space is not good," one person told me. "Bad omen."

I didn't realize how bad an omen it was.

Word quickly got around, and a steady stream of students came to my office to hold a vigil. They sat silently, as if they were in prayer or meditation. When they left, another group came to replace them. I wasn't able to get much work done that day. Shortly afterward, a teacher died and I was told it was witchcraft and the events were connected. Though I'm not superstitious, I decided to take things seriously even when I didn't understand the connection. It was part of living in Africa.

Thinking about the owl, I wondered about this mantis moving up the edge of the door. *Was this an omen?* Its presence changed the room. A few minutes earlier, I'd been sitting there alone and self-absorbed. Now the mantis had my complete attention.

The mantis in Bushmen lore was Kaggen, another trickster figure. Shape shifter, creator of illusion. *What was it that I was seeing? Was this a real mantis, or a mythical form?*

It was a measure of my state of fatigue and discouragement that I wanted the comfort of magical thinking. I needed more than cold hard reality. I didn't want to deal with scientific fact. I needed a sign — an omen — that my luck was changing.

Evening descended. The light shifted and the shadows lengthened. I'm not sure how long I'd gazed, transfixed, at the mantis, when my trance was interrupted by the sound of footsteps crunching in the sand. The noise startled me. When I looked up, I saw the man in blue coveralls approaching the open door. Moving quietly, he seemed to hold himself in the shade. It wasn't until he stepped out of the shadow that I was able to see him clearly.

He had white hair and a faint trace of a beard along his jaw. His small stature and profile gave him a slightly elfin look. He was barefoot. His coveralls were grimy and hung like a ragged curtain from his skinny frame. A gaping hole in his clothing exposed shrivel lines in his belly. I assumed his stomach had shrunk from hunger.

He stopped a few steps away and studied me in silence. His direct gaze made me feel like I was being examined. I sensed that my every move and facial expression was being recorded. I was being sized up.

"Dumelang, Tati." I greeted him as if he were an older man, though, in fact, he may have been ten years younger than me. His face was deeply lined from years of exposure to Kalahari sand and weather. As he moved into the light I noticed a puffiness around his eyes — too much alcohol?

Until I spoke, the man's hands hung loosely at his sides. Returning my greeting he clasped his hands prayerfully and bent his right knee in a stiff kind of curtsey. The greeting made me uncomfortable. I've always had a sense that the deferential curtsey had something to do with manners enforced under colonial rule. Besides, my own manners are nowhere near as gracious.

I expected to hear a greeting like dumela. Instead, the greeting was spoken with the accent of the western Kalahari — the "d" replaced with an "r," *"Rumela, Rra."*

The expression on his face did not change and his eyes did not relax their gaze.

He stopped near the front of the truck and propped his left arm against the bug screen. The top of his head barely reached the hood. There, between truck and hostel building, we regarded one another silently. I began to wonder how long the silence would last. In Africa, men can sit together for a long time without saying a word. But though the silence made me nervous, he seemed unperturbed.

Eventually, I had to speak. I wanted to ask him questions, even the simple kinds of questions that I could dredge up with my limited Setswana. What is your name? Where do you live? Where do you come from?

One question at a time, I checked myself.

His name was Sepeterus, at least that was the first name he gave me. But even a simple question can have a more complicated answer. Every farmer he had ever worked for had given him a different name. He had worked for black and white farmers. Besides Sepeterus, he had a string of Setswana given names. Sepeterus was a name assigned to him by an Afrikaner. White Boers were fond of giving African laborers Latin-sounding names.

Sepeterus pointed out his hut on the other side of the windmill, where I had seen him earlier. There had not been any rain in this village for a long time, but if there ever was, the shaggy thatch roof of his rondevaal looked as if it would be swamped.

He spoke no English and very little Setswana, but we were able to make ourselves understood. Sepeterus had traveled all over the desert. He had lived in the Ghanzi District and among the places he mentioned, I recognized the name of Xade, in the Central Kalahari. At one time he had hunted and lived a traditional Bushman life in the Central Kalahari. In Ghanzi, he had cared for herds and worked as a laborer.

Once again I stated the obvious in Setswana, "There is no rain."

Sepeterus replied in Setswana, *"Pula ga e o."* There is no rain. Then he surprised me by repeating a Nharo phrase that sounded to me like, *"tun ka."* I did not understand at first, but he persisted and made me understand that "tun ka," meant "there is no rain."

Then, with gestures and pointing, Sepeterus taught me a few Nharo words, managing to get me to pronounce the sounds for bush and tree.

The herd of small goats moved across the red sand grazing under the shade of a low acacia. Sepeterus pointed them out and taught me the word for goat. Then he pointed to a small puffy cloud in the sky, to buildings, and to other objects around us. I tried to say the words as he repeated them. I imitated his pronunciation and then forgot the words as quickly as he pointed to the next thing.

He anticipated my problems in pronunciation and repeated sounds for me. If I'd been a linguist or an anthropologist, he'd be a perfect teacher. I was neither, but he was just what I needed at that moment.

We stood in front of the truck, pointing at bushes and trees and he even managed a smile. Not exactly a smile that conveyed any sort of inner pleasure, but rather a smile that seemed to be aimed at making me feel comfortable. On Sepeterus's face, likely unused to emotional display, the smile was a feat of coordination requiring noticeable effort. His instincts were correct, however. I felt more at ease than I had thirty minutes earlier.

Finally there seemed to be nothing more to say, and I knew there was a fair exchange required. For every service performed, there is a *quid pro quo.*

I had already seen the shrivel lines across the man's belly and I knew he was probably hungry.

I reached into the truck and from the food box brought out what I needed. Within minutes, I was watching the butane burner heat water for powdered soup. Sepeterus, hunkered in a natural crouch, his feet flat on the ground, elbows on his knees, tore away at a loaf of French bread we'd purchased just that morning from a bakery in Maun.

Then Gen's face appeared from behind the truck — she hadn't yet noticed Sepeterus. "I found the kitchen," she said.

Sepeterus finished eating and left as silently as he'd arrived. I turned to put cooking utensils away and when I looked back, he was gone. But my spirits had risen considerably. I wanted to show Gen the mantis, but it, too, had disappeared and was now nowhere in sight.

I entered the drab dorm room to put away my notebook before we headed over to the kitchen to cook supper. As my steps resounded on the hard surface of the narrow dorm room, and I looked at the cones of mosquito netting hung over our twin cots, my pack, and the familiar belongings on the bed, I realized that while I was not in Ghanzi, I was in the Ghanzi District. I tossed my notebook on the bed and realized that physically I'd been in Dkar for half a day, but mentally, I'd just arrived. I felt a silent sigh of relief.

Tomorrow morning, I said to myself, *I'll inquire about Freddy just to see if anyone knows him or has heard of him.*

The white walls of the tiny kitchen glared with the reflected light of a fluorescent tube. Gen boiled rice in the same pan I'd used that morning to make tea. When it was ready, she scrambled in a couple of eggs, purchased in Maun. I sat in a plastic chair across from a sparkling white stove, telling her about my intention to ask about Freddy.

When we were both seated, eating from our enameled plates, she asked, "What are the chances?"

"It's worth asking. A flip of the coin."

After dinner, we put everything into the back of the truck in preparation to leave in the morning. I washed the dishes in a deep stainless steel sink and stacked them in a box. Gen made several trips to store food in the truck. After one of her trips to the truck, I heard the sound of women's voices and laughter outside. Gen had made friends earlier with a couple of middle-aged cleaning women as they worked around the hostel. A few minutes later, she walked into the kitchen with a strange expression on her face. I couldn't tell what was going on. Either she was about to burst into tears or was excited. I couldn't tell which.

Gen began speaking in questions. "One of the women? A housekeeper who works here?"

What was she trying to say?

Her words came out in a rush and she continued without stopping to take a breath. "Her last name is Morris, she told me. Married to one of Freddy's sons. Talk to the woman at Kuru Centre in the morning. She'll be able to give you directions."

13 Looking into the Lens

I could hardly believe it. In the morning I was too excited to eat. The moment had arrived. We'd traveled across the Kalahari to try to locate Freddy and today I hoped I was going to meet him.

It was eight-thirty in the morning and already I knew the day would be hot. I gulped my tea and grabbed my tape recorder and writing pad. The sun was low in the sky as I headed to the zebra-striped store. Outside, brown dust hung thick in the slanting light. Five minutes earlier a truck on the way from Ghanzi to Maun had driven past and left the air smelling dusty and dry.

The blond lady in the store was working with a Nharo woman stacking cans on a shelf behind the counter. As I entered, she paused to tick off items on a clipboard. The other woman was clearly San. She wore a heavy gray sweatshirt and her hair was wrapped with a yellow-print scarf.

I asked the blond woman about Freddy and, instead of giving me an answer, she turned to her co-worker and said something in Nharo. I listened to her speaking with the soft clicks that sounded like pebbles and rustling leaves, and I remembered the quiet speech of the Dzu Twasi in the Tsodilo Hills. But she gave me no confirmation as to whether Freddy lived in Dkar or whether he was alive.

The Nharo woman left the store. "She's gone to get Mr. Morris's daughter," the woman said at last. "Liza will take you."

Where will she take me? I wondered. *To Freddy's? To where he actually stays? Or to someone who will explain the facts of his dying? I would find out soon enough.*

I said, "You speak Nharo. I'm surprised."

"I have lived here all my life," she said with careful English grammar. "I learned to speak Nharo before I knew English." She laughed, "I didn't know English until I went to school in Ghanzi. I am speaking to you in my third language."

She said it with a certain amount of pride. Like someone saying, "My grades were straight As in my senior year." Of course, her attitude was a result of her pride of ancestry. She was pure Afrikaner, proud of the fact that she didn't speak English until she needed to.

A door opened in the back of the store and another woman entered. Thirtyish and petite, she had light skin and black hair in tight peppercorn curls. Her dark eyes revealed nothing. She and the blond woman exchanged a few words in Nharo. The younger woman did not look in my direction, nor did she smile. But the blond woman turned and said to me, "Follow her."

Out the door we went, walking east into the morning sun. Retracing the rocky and dusty road that brought me here.

Though we had not been introduced, I assumed that the woman I walked with was Liza.

I remembered the photograph in the small book I'd found in the University of Botswana Library in Gaborone that showed a white man, Freddy, seated with his family around him. His wife was standing by his side, holding a small child. Near his knee, two older children — a girl and a boy — stared back at the photographer, curious yet obviously impatient. Which child was Liza? The one in her mother's arms or the one standing beside her father?

The camera had shown Freddy looking directly into the lens, a broad-shouldered strong man with large hardworking hands comfortably at rest on his lap. Even in the shade under a wide-brimmed hat, his eyes gave off a light. At seventy-five, he radiated an attitude: "I'm a man to deal with."

Today, Liza set a brisk pace down the sandy road and past the white-washed buildings of an elementary school where women workers shoveled wet concrete for a construction crew. Barefoot and silent, Liza maintained a long stride. We covered a lot of distance in a hurry, speeding past the school and the surrounding low, chain-link fence.

Facing into the bright sun, we headed toward a cluster of tall acacia thorns. With the sun in my eyes, I couldn't make out details, but a group of huts were silhouetted in the shadows.

Liza led me into a compound where the earth was streaked with light and shadow. After walking for several minutes in complete silence, she finally spoke.

I was too startled to understand. I wanted to ask her what she'd said, but before I could get the words out, she'd already turned and was walking back in the direction we had come.

I decided that Liza had said, "Freddy stays here."

Blinded by the sunlight, I could only see the shapes of trees and houses. After a minute, my eyes began to adjust. Then I saw three square mud houses. The nearest hut had a corrugated metal roof held down with stones. Flaking mud walls exposed the mud blocks underneath, and the hinged door hung aslant. Beyond the other two buildings, under the largest thorn tree, a cooking area was screened off by a stick fence.

Shading my eyes with my hand, I walked directly into the sunlight toward the center of the compound, where two chairs were placed side by side next to a low wooden bench.

My stomach was in knots. My shoulders felt weighted down with a ton of expectations I'd carried across the desert. A hundred questions ran through my mind and I felt the urge to blurt them all out. It had been almost two years since I had traveled to the Tsodilo Hills. Two years since my illusions about the San had been shattered. I wanted to know more about the San culture. When I first read about Freddy in the newspaper months ago, I saw a ray of hope. *Am I really going to meet him? And if I do, is it going to lead to some understanding, or give me a way of knowing Bushmen as real people, not just exotic beings that I'd read about in textbooks?* I wanted reality. I wanted to shed my romantic notions.

Again I remembered the photo of Freddy with his family. The way his eyes seemed to burn with intensity. Now it was my turn to look. I had to see, understand, and listen. There was too much in my mind that expected something unreal.

The newspaper article I'd read months earlier had described Freddy as a white Bushman. *How much of that was factual? Had Freddy really lived with the Bushmen as a hunter? Had he hunted with bows? Had he worn furs? How much could he really tell me about hunting in the old days?*

The light was still playing tricks, and it wasn't until I was quite close to the seating area that I saw a man sitting hunched over in one of the chairs. When I first saw him, I thought he was sleeping. Then I saw that he was fumbling with a plastic bag on his lap.

With arthritic fingers, he was trying to put tubes of salve and medicine into the bag and tie it. He wore a threadbare, checkered suit jacket. His hat appeared to be brown felt, the nap worn dark and caked black with years of dust and perspiration. At some time in the past, the crown of the hat had been repaired with what looked to be brown packing tape.

The old man had not yet looked up and I didn't want to catch him by surprise. I didn't know what to expect. He might tell me to go away. I walked carefully — a hesitant petitioner hoping for an audience with an elderly man under a flat-topped acacia tree. I suddenly noticed that my morning tea had left a sour taste in my mouth.

"Hello," I said, and took another step. "Freddy Morris?"

He looked up, trying to focus cloudy blue eyes on whoever was speaking. After several seconds, his weathered brown face crinkled into a smile.

"Yah, sit down," he said in a thick Afrikaans or Dutch accent, motioning me toward the rickety wooden bench where I took a seat. He returned to his task of wrapping up his medicine and said nothing for several minutes. Finally, he got up from his aluminum chair, carried the bag to the crooked door of one of the mud houses, and disappeared inside. After a minute, he reemerged without the bag, shuffled across the flat brown sand, and settled himself back into the ragged seat of his chair.

"I not feeling so nice these days. My knees are sore." He bent over and pulled up his trousers to show me his swollen left knee. His feet were in high-topped shoes without socks. At the ankles, his skin was dark and cracked from years of sun. At the middle of his shin, his skin was white as ash and his blue veins made a highway map. I could see that his left knee was inflamed.

"My legs hurt all the time." Freddy adjusted his trouser leg and settled back. "Mmph," he grunted as he tried to move his sore legs into a comfortable position. Freddy seemed to have grown smaller over the years. His checkered suit jacket hung loosely and his hat rested on his ears.

Nearby, utensils and plates rattled and clanged, and for the first time, my attention was drawn to another part of the living area, where Freddy's wife washed enameled metal dishes and pots in a plastic tub of soapy water. Then she stacked the plates on a board. She was dressed in what appeared to be her bed clothes, a T-shirt with a loose sarong wrapped around her waist. She had not yet tied up her black hair with a scarf or bandana.

I wondered if it were possible that she was forty years younger than Freddy? Then the answer came to me. Yes. Possibly, she was even fifty years younger than her husband.

Freddy and I sat across from one another. I searched for something to talk about. At first, he seemed delighted to have company, but soon he began to fidget as if his chair was suddenly uncomfortable or his pant leg too tight.

I was facing the reality of the man himself: his checkered jacket, slacks, shoes, and Western style hat. He looked more like a Dutch farmer than a white Bushman. I realized I should have expected this, but I hadn't. *What had I expected? Had I exchanged one romantic notion for another? Had I stopped idealizing the Bushman, only to begin idealizing the life of a white Bushman?*

I counseled myself to wait patiently in order to hear Freddy tell me his story. But I wrestled to control my anticipation for something more ideal than real. The ideal was a story of a Western man who had returned to a traditional way of life — a life more pure, morally superior to life in the modern world. In my tale, Freddy played the leading role.

For several minutes, I looked around. My mind turned to mush as I felt my expectations butt head-on into reality. I was worried the entire meeting would turn into a disaster. But finally, I was able to speak. Looking for a place to begin, I asked, "Is all this your compound?"

"No, this Liza's. Where she stays." Freddy motioned toward a round mud hut with a neat thatch roof. An unfinished rectangular structure of poles and mud daub appeared to be under construction. "She wants a metal roof on this one," he said, pointing to the rectangular building.

Then he looked over at the closest structure; its two doors were barely hanging on and the mud was falling off the bricks in chunks. "This wants to fall over. But it can't. I need to live here." Freddy chuckled at his joke.

He gazed around for a minute, like a farmer studying the sky for signs of weather. "Mmph," the grunting sound again, from deep in his throat. "The rain this-a year is very scarce."

His accent was a mix of Dutch and African, and his missing teeth caused him to mumble. I had to ask him to repeat himself until I understood what he'd said.

"The rain this year is very scarce. Very dry. Making clouds, but there is only wind. Only wind. Only wind." Freddy tilted back in his chair and scanned the deep-blue sky overhead. On the wooden bench, I leaned forward with the effort to attune myself to Freddy's manner of speaking.

"Too dry. And it's not only this year. From last year. Very dry also."

He talked as if I were just another Dutch farmer who happened by to pass the time of day. If I were Dutch, Freddy could have spoken Afrikaans. Plainly, he was not comfortable with English. It wasn't his first language and Freddy's use of English was influenced by all the languages he spoke. I could hear Dutch grammar in the phrase "Making clouds, but there is only wind." Like an African speaker, he exaggerated his vowels, wrapping his lips around the sound, and lavishly rolled every "r."

"I see only clouds. Not rain. Clouds blow back, all the time. Clouds shouldn't go one side to the other side. Come from this side. Come from this side. The winds can bring the clouds from any direction. But then the clouds must stay. They must stay and make big clouds and rain. You think it will rain, but it won't rain. The ground staying dry, dry, dry. Night. Day. Dry, staying dry. The soil turns to dust."

The Nharo intensify meaning by repetition. In English we would say "very dry," but Nharo speakers say "dry, dry, dry."

I listened to Freddy talk about weather and uncertainty. The drought had continued for two years, but he had seen drought before. Every decade had its periods without regular rains. He had lived with uncertain weather all his life. He was not really complaining. Instead, his comments seemed consistent with an African way of understanding. I understood his talk about weather as an effort to understand by asking himself questions: "What do the unseen powers have in store for us now? What obstacles will they throw up before us? We must always be observant, never feel too comfortable."

The talk about weather helped me quiet my mind. Sitting with Freddy, I needed some time to relax. I had anticipated this meeting for a long time and now it had come so suddenly, I didn't feel prepared. My stomach felt unsettled. I heard a quaver in my voice. I tried to relax by reminding myself that there would be more to come — more conversation, I had only just arrived.

My stomach tingled with excitement. I leaned forward on my bench seat. *I was actually here with Freddy Morris!*

The silver tips of his whiskers made a thorny surface on his brown cracked skin. Seeing the man before me, I was still in disbelief. Torn between the real and the ideal, I studied the man's grizzled face and the clothes draped loosely over his once massive frame.

Freddy was born with white skin, but his face was now browned from the harsh rays of the sun, and mottled by sores that had formed and then healed. I'd seen the same dry, mottled appearance on the skin of other creatures of the desert. Years earlier, there may have been more people like him, men of European descent who found shelter in this harsh environment, but now he had outlived others of his kind.

I asked if he had farmed here, in this area.

Everything looked so dry and parched, I doubted a farm could be successful.

He took my question literally to mean, the very ground where we sit. "No, across the road there," he said, pointing to where a flock of goats were grazing. "Where the goats are, you can see. Making nice vegetable."

The ruminants, the same ones I had seen a day earlier, browsed among thorny shrubs.

"Yes, you can working with the pump. From borehole." Freddy pointed in the direction of a building to the west of where we sat. "Two big tanks. That's water from the borehole in those tanks. Everybody gets water there. But this is alright, borehole works. So, everybody has water."

We had talked for forty-five minutes, then during a pause I asked, "Freddy, I understand that you grew up with the Nharo."

The question was couched as a statement; I hoped that he'd free associate. What I really wanted was confirmation of a myth: the story of the white man who became a Bushman. I hoped he would tell me Nharo stories enriched with the names of his Nharo contemporaries.

"Yes, yes, all the boys were Nharo. Christian LaVish *vass de only ooder*," — was the only other — he said. "Do you know him?"

I didn't know him, of course. Freddy was used to a community where everyone knew everybody else.

"Others were also Dutch — Drotsky, Ver Nierden, all your old Dutch people were staying near Ghanzi. My father was the only Scots." He paused, and then remembered, "There was Hardbattle, he was Scots. Tom Hardbattle and my father, only the two Scots people in the area. A lot of Dutch.

Makokus, de la Bushie, LaVish, Lambke. Brunwalt was a German. The black people that lived there were the Barolongs."

Hardbattle was the only name I recognized. But the friends he mentioned were all of European descent. I didn't press him, but I wasn't satisfied with the answer.

Freddy's gnarled hands lay folded on his lap as he spoke. We sat under a thorn tree in Africa, but it could have been a Bodhi tree in India. Two men — elderly sage and seeker. As the sage slumped in his aluminum folding chair, the seeker, perched on a bench, tried to sort out truth from his own fantasy.

Around us, the others who lived in the compound carried on with their normal daily activities. Near the edge of the compound a rooster crowed and a flock of chickens pecked at the sandy earth. Freddy's wife knelt in the cooking area and blew into the embers of a smoldering mophane log, sending a thin column of blue smoke into the air. The yard was filled with a sharp, sweet mahogany fragrance. Porridge steamed under the lid of a large enameled pot she had set off to one side. Occasionally, she glanced maternally toward two toddlers playing nearby, making sure they didn't get too close to the flame. As Freddy's wife worked, she paid no attention to us. In the San culture, men have their world; women have theirs.

She placed a kettle of hot water over the renewed flames just as five children in school uniforms — girls in maroon, boys in dark blue, all of them with Nharo features — streamed into the yard from the elementary school I had passed earlier. The schoolchildren, home for their morning tea, lined up in a stair step by age. I guessed the oldest was twelve and the youngest seven. To prepare for the meal, they rinsed their metal plates in a plastic tub on a board near the fire. I had seen the kids at the school where I'd taught rinse their dishes this way before they ate.

I watched the activity in the yard and thought about the transformation of a man from white Afrikaner to Bushman. Then I rephrased the question I had asked earlier into a more specific series of questions.

"What can you tell me about the hunting in those days? Did you live as a hunter? Did you hunt with bows? How did you hunt?" I wanted stories of poisoned arrow tips. I wanted him to share the secrets of stalking antelope in the desert.

"My father got a shotgun and a Mauser. I can't say what the number is. A Mauser rifle." Freddy started to tell me something about the rifle, but whatever it was, he stopped talking when a young Nharo woman entered the yard, apparently on her way to talk to Freddy's wife. She made a detour to greet Freddy. Perhaps in her late teens or early twenties, she wore a red blouse and an ankle-length denim skirt. She walked over to us and greeted Freddy in Nharo and then gave me a formal curtsey and "Dumela."

I couldn't understand a word of their conversation, but it was more than just a "good morning-how are you?"

After his visitor left, Freddy shifted in his chair. "Mmph." It sounded as if he had to clear his throat in order to speak English.

Freddy started speaking again, and I realized I should just let him talk about anything. Just listen, I told myself.

"Yes. I can say I am born in Serowe. My father was a teacher in Serowe." He pronounced the name of the village, Serowe, with an impressive rolling of the "r," the African way. "Worked all over Botswana. My mother's family was from near Mafeking. They came up about the same time."

"They came up" was Afrikaner shorthand meaning that they had moved from South Africa.

"When would that have been? About 1900?" I asked.

"Oooh, a long time ago!" Apparently, the year didn't matter to him. But the fact he was born in Serowe interested me.

Serowe was the village of a famous Tswana chieftain, King Khama, also known as Khama the Good. I wanted to ask if his father knew Khama. A dozen other questions came to mind, but it wouldn't do any good to ask. Freddy would have been too young to be aware of those details.

Before he could continue, one of the schoolgirls walked in our direction carrying two metal cups of steaming tea. She was the eldest of the girls. With a silent curtsey, she placed the cups on a flat red stone near where we sat. The tea was white with scalded goat's milk and thick with sugar.

Freddy was still a baby when his father quit his teaching job in Serowe to become a trader and moved his family north. I asked Freddy where they lived before they came to Ghanzi.

"All over," he said. He went on to describe places in and around Maun. His father bought a shop in a village called Masire. "So we are staying there. I growing, getting to be a man now. Running around . . ."

Freddy paused and began to laugh. Something about that place recalled some fond memory, but he didn't explain.

"Then there come another man speaking with my father. His name is Becker. My father must give him the shop and butchery. My father think what is best, then he tell Mr. Becker, 'All right, but the money must balance. You must pay me fair price.' Shops, stuff, money, butcher shop brings in money. Yes! My father sold the shop then to Mr. Becker."

Telling the story of his father selling his business, Freddy became breathless with excitement as he placed the events in their proper sequence. "Yes!" he exclaimed. This was his stamp of approval to certify that the order was correct.

"Then we come from there, from Masire to Tsau. Old Captain Machibe, Batawana chief, was my father's friend. So, we are staying there, in Tsau with the Batawana and other groups of black people. Then Machibe going away to Maun. My father tell him, 'Yes, you throw me away and you go away. So now I going away to farm.' They were good friends. My father coming from Tsau."

Freddy coughed. "We came here when I was thirteen."

Freddy had mentioned two villages, Maun and Tsau. I had driven from Maun the day before, and Tsau was just west of Maun on the way to Dkar, a few miles north of where we had picked up the hitchhikers. He didn't have the historical markers to anchor the times, but I guessed that Freddy had followed the route about eighty years earlier, close to the beginning of World War I — 1913 or 1914.

After he told me about his family living in villages all around the Okavango and Maun, and then eventually moving to Tsau and then Ghanzi, there was a long pause. I picked up the light-blue metal cup and tested the temperature of the rim before I took a sip of my tea.

I suddenly remembered a news story I'd seen in Gaborone and set my cup down. "Freddy, did you hear that a lion near Tsau killed a child? Just a few weeks ago."

"Lions can do it lots of times. They can kill five people, or six people. When we live in Maun, a lion was killing cattle. We got a group to take his spoor and get that lion. Chase him up. Then he chase us. We run away with the horses. We was eight people. All of us had guns. Some go this way, others go that way."

I imagined the chaotic scene: a posse in disarray and eight people scrambling to escape on horseback.

"Alright, the lion coming in, going after the chief's son. He chase us on the horses and get him up on the back. Jumped up on the horse and he take that man and put him down. And then all of these people was chasing away. The lion bit his leg here. Off. Broken." Freddy pointed to his upper leg.

"He crying, saying, 'Help me. Help me.' Other people too fright to coming back. I coming back there and jumping off my horse. I take my gun and I standing over the man. The gun barrel, I put it just here by the lion." Freddy placed his index finger between his eyes. "And I shoot him in. He still hold the Tswana man. I take my gun barrel and put it in his mouth. The lion still got the man. And I take my gun and I broke the lion's mouth open."

"You had to do that to relax his jaw?"

"And then I get him out."

"Your friend's leg — bitten off? Did he live?"

"Yes, we take him back to Maun. He walking with stick — crutch."

"Which chief was that?"

"Machibe"

"Machibe, your father's friend?"

"Yes."

"That must have been a long time ago."

"Aii! At that time I was a nice big pony. We move after that."

When he finished, I was still not sure whether the man's leg had been bitten off or simply broken. But that was not the important part of the story for me. Freddy was probably twelve years old. Killing a lion and saving the life of his friend, the chief's son, sounded like Freddy's initiation into manhood. I let the image sink in. Thinking of the photograph I'd seen, I remembered the fire in his eyes. His eyes full of intensity and conviction. *Was that the expression of a man who has faced a lion without backing down?*

Freddy finished his tea and grew silent for a minute. I heard his feet scrape on the earth and saw him struggle to escape from his chair. With delicate steps, he shuffled toward a triple-strand of barbed wire fence near the road. Once he reached the fence, he peed through the barbed wire, splashing into the sand.

When he had settled back in his chair, I asked, "How old are you?"

"I'm a hundred and twenty." His manner was brash and aggressive, challenging me to contradict him.

I knew he was not 120. He could be ninety-five. But I had asked a pointless question about something obvious. By his answer he meant, *Can't you see I'm old?*

"A man your age, you look to be in very good health," I said.

"Yes. Only this year my knees is getting sore. Horse was falling with me. I riding the horse and then he jump and jump and after, he fall. When he fall, his head underneath and nearly take me with him. Knee was out. That was last year."

What was a man as old as Freddy doing on a horse? I wondered. But I kept silent.

"Now, it's only that knee," he pointed to his left knee. "That one. The other one, it's okay. Only the left knee what worries me." Freddy paused. "And my eyes don't want to see no more. Sun coming up and the whole country is only one smoke," he laughed. "Only smoke out there. You can't see what is what, and what is what. You see a man, it's like a pole."

The children across the yard were chatty and animated. They stood or leaned against a tree trunk eating the porridge that had been ladled onto their plates. Cups of tea were lined up in a row on a nearby log. The older girls were already rinsing their dishes and getting ready to go back to school.

Listening to Freddy and watching the children, I asked, "Freddy, how many children do you have?"

"Aii!" He counted on his fingers and tried to come up with names. Struggling with the answer he began to count some fingers twice. The effort went on for so long, I almost felt guilty for throwing out such a difficult problem.

He had to start over. This time counting wives rather than children.

"The one girl, I gotting by her four sons. Then she crooking me."

"You mean that woman left you?"

"Not left me. She sleep with another man. When I found out I said, 'No *mon*, there can't be two men with one girl. So, I will get out. You can stay with him.' "

Her name was Nxuya. Freddy clicked his tongue pronouncing the name. "She stays near Morris. Morris, my big son." He held his left hand in the air and lifted a second finger. "And the other one. How many she have?" He counted on the same hand, but didn't manage a result.

"Third one, she was bad luck. I got only two children with her. A son and a daughter. But the daughter going and the mother also."

His daughter going? She died. And his wife, as well. "Yes, bad luck," I said.

"So, I staying here, two years, then I take this one." Freddy nodded toward the cooking area in the compound where his wife worked. "Xotlay. Our oldest daughter, Liza."

Freddy struggled to remember names of other children. I knew some of his children were in their sixties. "How many? Two . . ."

A truck roared past on the road and stirred up a cloud of dust.

". . . Liza, Freddy, and then, one is also going away. I've buried two children. Then two sisters. Five. Six. Then two little children. The little one is my last." Freddy pointed across the yard. A naked little girl about three years of age had just had a bath and stood clinging to her mother's leg. She had fair skin and blond curly hair. "That's all. Finished."

I had put him on the spot and as far as I could tell, he had not been able to count all the children. In his telling, I had counted four wives and many offspring. That was my way of seeing the world — my cultural assumption — quantitative answers, ages or numbers of children. But for Freddy the story of wives and children was not about ages or numbers at all. It was a personal drama of loyalty, infidelity, and loss. The answer had more to do with his heart than a number. So I tried to help out, "You must have about twenty children altogether."

"Yes," Freddy laughed, sounding much relieved. "Yes," he said as he started coughing again. "They can be staying nice on these farms."

"It's a good place to raise children, on a farm." I used his word "farm," although I could see nothing farm-like about the place.

The sun had moved across the sky and the shade had moved away from us. He squinted. "Is the sun in your eyes?" I asked.

We both stood up and I shifted the chairs out of the sun. I couldn't shift the bench because it rested on several rocks. After kicking aside some rocks on the ground, we pushed the bases of our chairs into the sand.

"Stony. Stony. Stony. The whole place is stones," Freddy said. "Where there's no stones, gardens are good. Big watermelon. Big pumpkin."

I hoped he'd be willing to talk more about his childhood.

"Do you still remember your friends as a young man?" He had mentioned Dutch names; I hoped he'd name some Nharo companions.

"How you mean? Only the ones we staying with. Not call everyone our friends."

"You learned the language."

"Weak. Weak. I only learning by talking it. I can talk it. I can talk it just like my own language." He was skirting my question and wouldn't give me a direct answer. I wondered whether he didn't understand or whether the avoidance was deliberate.

In the two hours that I'd sat with Freddy, a parade of visitors came through his yard. They seemed to be drawn by an atmosphere of gentleness and paternal care. The young people who visited certainly felt that. The strong man's power had diminished since the photograph I'd seen in Gaborone was taken, but not his ability to take people under his wing. He seemed to be a father figure for many people here.

Most of his visitors spoke Nharo and I listened to the gentle clicking speech. Others from the village spoke Setswana with Freddy. I eavesdropped on the conversations without understanding a word. The visitors were all people from the village. I didn't count them, but I paid attention to the languages they spoke. I overheard one conversation in Afrikaans. Some of the Nharo sat without speaking, apparently, just to hear us speak English. I was a stranger and seemed to be a source of interest. After each visitor, Freddy turned and made a sound from deep in his chest, "Mmph," before we resumed.

Where Freddy lived, it was not unusual for a person to speak four different languages, but I continued to be impressed by his linguistic ability. The ability to switch from one language to another seems amazing to a person from the US where English is the only language needed. When I commented on it, he offered his "Mmph" and minimized the accomplishment, saying, "I know from speaking only. Not from books."

Freddy seemed to be growing tired. The man was still a paradox for me and there was still more of his story I wanted to learn. But at least I felt closer to some of the answers.

"Can I come to see you tomorrow?"

"Yes," he said.

"I'll bring you some aspirin."

His face lit up with a toothless smile. "Oh, that's nice medicine."

The sky was cloudless. The air was hot. Freddy looked around at nothing in particular, perhaps scanning the sky for signs, or else reviewing in his mind the range of our conversation.

When he spoke, his words were not addressed to me. He looked into the distance, as if there was someone else present, some trickster who played with age and years and was able to conjure up past events at will.

"That's a long time," he said. There was wonder in Freddy's voice.

14 Hunter

Until that day, the Freddy in my mind was the man in the photograph with his Nharo wife and his children. It surprised me how accurate that picture was. The whole time I sat with Freddy, his wife and several children were always in the vicinity.

As I left his compound to walk back toward our hostel, I remembered the day I first read about Freddy. I'd felt sure that meeting him would open a door leading to a direct experience with the San culture. Walking away, I told myself that at least I had met him. Despite feeling puzzled and vaguely unsatisfied by some of his responses, I was willing to allow for the rest to unfold.

I retraced the steps I'd followed with Freddy's daughter Liza that morning. As I passed the elementary school, I noticed that Dkar felt like a different place than it had yesterday.

Everyone I saw was busy. There were development projects taking place all over the village. At a preschool, I saw children playing organized games in an open yard. They sang out, "One, two, three . . .." I walked past a tannery where the air smelled like shoe dye, and men were crafting leather products out of thick animal hide. In another building, women were gathered in a crafts room to sew. Quilt fragments lay strewn on the floor and the air hummed with the quiet murmur of conversation.

Near the road, I passed a vegetable garden growing under shade netting with a drip irrigation system. And next to the garden, in bright sunlight, prickly pear cactus grew behind a fence. The cactus pads were covered with cochineal, tiny insects that produce a red dye. All of these activities were economic development projects established by the Kuru Development Trust for the San people.

Further along I stopped at the crafts shop in the Kuru Centre to look at a display of utensils, toys, carvings, leather work, and a variety of hunting kits on sale that had been made by members of the community. I put down my small backpack on the counter and browsed through the shop.

A young man in a chair bantered in Setswana with a woman across the room. She was folding T-shirts with silk-screened designs and stacking them on shelves. When she finished, she left, and the man turned to help me. I paid for a few items I'd picked out, including a pouch decorated with ostrich shell beads. It was made of soft leather and had a wide shoulder strap.

I asked the man, "Could you teach me something about this?"

"Teach you about it?" he said in English. "You mean the Nharo words?"

That was what I wanted. I was confident the pouch was a genuine artifact. A practical item of great usefulness.

"We call it *dobay*. It is made with ostrich shell, *qkoray*." He pronounced qkoray with a hard click, and then looked at me expecting me to repeat it."

I couldn't tell how he made the click sound. "A click with a 'k' sound, you use those together?" I asked. "That's very difficult for me."

He then pointed to the thread and stated the obvious, "This makes the beads stick to the leather. You sew the ostrich shell bead, *aba*."

When he said aba, I heard another kind of click, a sucking sound, made between his cheek and his teeth.

"These small bits of leather," he said as he held the thongs that hung from the bottom of the pouch, "we call them *kweray*."

"How would you use this in Nharo culture?" I asked, expecting him to say something about traditional medicine. Or about herbs to ward off spells and sorcery.

"It is a special bag," he said. I felt confirmed. I had made the right choice. "You know these bags, they can be used for putting things like radios in." I felt deflated. "When you are going for a tour, you can use this bag to put other things in." He reached over to my small pile of artifacts and picked one up. "You see, you can put this one inside this one and carry it around your neck."

His comment seemed so simple, I thought he must be putting me on. But he had observed me entering with my backpack and I had a sudden insight into the way he looked upon the culture of white-skinned travelers. The salesman was showing me the value and convenience of the useless things I'd purchased. He knew whites carried lots of extra belongings and were fond of carrying weights around their necks. He'd seen that Westerners like to put one thing inside another thing. The outer bag or container was useless except to carry the thing inside. He knew I was going to put everything inside my pack when we finished talking. More than likely, when I got back to the hostel, I'd put my pack in a box and then, before we left, I'd put the box in the back of the truck. At home, I'd put everything on my wall to gather dust.

"What's your name?" I asked.

"I am Hunter. That is my English name." He told me his name was Kakwe in Nharo and Galetsaole in Setswana. His father was Zambian and his mother, Nharo.

Hunter went on to say that in Dkar he was working to improve his understanding of Nharo and to "understand what I am as a Nharo."

"You're learning about Nharo culture?"

"Many of us study Nharo life. The people now, they have changed," Hunter said.

"The childrens don't know how to hunt," he said. "The old mens who know how to hunt can teach us. We will go the Wildlife or the Game and ask for permission if we can go and hunt with bows and arrows. Then if we find animals, we can shoot and see how that is working."

I decided his mention of "the Wildlife or the Game" must refer to the Ministry of Wildlife or the Ministry of Game.

"In other words, young people will learn hunting skills from the old men," I replied

"Yeah. Also, we have been having the workshop of dancing."

"Dancing workshop?" My Western mind immediately pictured an absurd scene of couples in ballroom poses with waltz music playing. Then I remembered the chanting and the rhythms of the trance dance I'd heard at Nata.

"We have a feast," he continued. "After eating meat in the evening, men put on their rattles, then they dance. Everybody dance for the whole night. Until the sun is up. We have done that the passing year. We are going to do more."

"Trance dance healing?" It seemed like a revelation to me. The trance dances were being taught in order to perpetuate the custom.

"Yeah, trance dances. That is the purpose. Sometimes there can be someone who is sick in the family. Then traditional doctors in the family help that sick person. So, they used to dance and dance and dance. They can help that person heal."

I left Hunter in the store and walked away with a strange feeling of anticipation. *Would it be possible for me to witness a healing dance?* I hadn't even asked about it, but a new possibility was beginning to appear.

Gen was resting in our hostel room when I returned at about 11 a.m., and we decided to walk over to the kitchen for an early lunch. She set out ingredients for a do-it-yourself sandwich, and I made juice out of orange concentrate. "Squash" was the word used for orange concentrate in this part of the world.

"I talked with the two women who work here, Bareng and Frederika," Gen said. She was slicing a baguette and placing enameled plates on the small table. "Bareng is the cook."

We sat down to eat and Gen continued, "I asked Bareng, 'Are we taking your job away from you by doing our own cooking?' She said, 'No, I don't know what food to fix white people. I don't know how you eat. I don't know what to cook for white people.'"

Gen spread her baguette with mayonnaise.

"So, I asked her, 'Do you want to see what I made for supper last night?' I took them in the kitchen and gave them some leftover pumpkin soup. Both liked it and wanted to know how I made it. I gave them a list of ingredients."

I poured our juice into enameled cups on the table.

Gen went on, "Bareng told me she would use the recipe. We also talked about gardening. She has a garden plot where she grows carrots, maize . . . a variety of veggies. Frederika was interested when I described my herb garden."

We ate silently for a minute, finishing our lunch, then Gen remembered something. "I found the art studio," she said. "You won't believe it."

"I won't? Why is that?"

"Remember the exhibit I saw in Gaborone?"

"At the National Gallery? I remember you describing an exhibit of baskets."

"That's right. And in another part of the gallery there was a show of Bushman contemporary paintings."

"Okay. I do remember you mentioned that."

"Well, guess what? The artists represented in that show live here in Dkar and work in the studio."

"Did you meet them?"

"Not really — there were language barriers. But I watched them work for a while. I didn't have my camera with me, or I would have taken pictures. Want to go? I'll bring my camera this time."

A tree shaded the entrance to the art studio, which, like the hostel, was a varnished log structure. Several carpenters worked at the far end of the building. They stood amid saw horses, tools, and pieces of wood. Either they were repairing something or it was still under construction. Two Nharo women danced outside. Each wore a colorful head scarf, cotton blouse, and wrap skirt. The two women were artists finding their inspiration in dance.

Inside paintings were stacked against walls and several painters were working at easels. To the right three people were chatting in an office.

I stuck my head in the door to ask permission to visit and take photographs. They invited us in and we introduced ourselves. The group included a white couple from South Africa, who were there to help facilitate the art program, and a Nharo woman, named Tukwa, who was a translator.

The man explained that the Dkar artists had exhibited their work in several large cities, including Johannesburg, Cape Town, and London.

"Sales of the paintings bring income to the artists. Ninety percent of the revenue goes to the artist and the other ten to the Kuru Foundation," he explained. "The goal is to encourage artists to produce a visual communication of their culture. We have not given the artists any class in composition or color. But the artists have traveled to the Tsodilo Hills and other places to see traditional Bushman art."

Tukwa offered to show us through the studio. With the help of her translations, I asked the artists questions, while Gen took pictures.

One artist stopped painting and stood stiffly near his easel when we approached. I asked him to tell me about his painting. Tukwa translated his answer, "It's a chameleon, a scorpion, and a lizard. At night the lizard makes a chk-chk-chk sound."

"I've heard them," I said.

At the next easel, the artist pointed to the tsama melons on the canvas. The melons grow in the desert. In the painting, they were part of a beautiful geometric design in desert colors — sage green and earthy orange-brown.

I could see what the couple meant about communicating aspects of the culture visually. In vivid color, the artists depicted their observations of life in the desert and the themes of their tales.

He had another painting of rain that showed storks sitting in a tree. "They come in the rain," the artist said. The painting reminded me of the morning we watched storks circle outside the home of our friend Marjorie.

"And here are frogs," he explained. The four frogs stood like small green men in a wide-open stance, arms spread.

Another artist, Tomas, was working just outside the door of the studio. His large canvas leaned against a wall while he filled in details from his seat on a low metal stool. Against a deep-blue background, a large horned animal with a red mouth dominated the field. Tomas explained that his painting depicted a tale in the Nharo culture. "This is a cow-person telling a story," he said. "The story is about the goat. It's a goat that doesn't live on a farm. It travels at night and eats people's heads. This goat is an animal you do not want to meet."

The two women we had seen dancing in front of the building had lined up several pictures along the outer wall of the studio. One of them held the top of a large painting, which rested on the concrete floor. It showed a fanciful village with traditional grass houses placed on the limbs of trees. The domes of the huts were an abstract checkerboard of pink, yellow, and blue.

"There is a jackal," she said. "The wild animals are in the trees along with the houses. It's a mongongo tree."

The other woman had also arranged several canvases on the concrete walk outside. She pointed to one with a strong non-representational design of red, yellow, and green. A desert shrub grew in the foreground. "This picture shows the different foods women gather," she explained. "Roots from the desert. The women are going out to gather the foods. There are the eggs of the birds. A tree and a springhare." She showed us several more paintings, all with geometric designs using shape and color.

Gen was excited about the abstract paintings. We thanked Tukwa for her translation, and as we left Gen observed, "There was no recognizable subject in those pictures. Yet they had a certain power. Those paintings drew you in and made you feel you were part of the work. Did you notice?"

I hadn't had time to digest what I'd seen. "I liked them," I said, "but I don't think I could explain it."

"Technically excellent," Gen said. "The compositions showed an understanding. The artists are all talented. I especially liked the paintings by the woman who did the abstractions . . . she knew what she was doing. Hers were powerful."

As we walked back toward the hostel, Gen was silent for a while, then said, "It makes you wonder, what's the source? . . . It may be that the source is the trance state. Remember the rock paintings we saw in the Tsodilo Hills? Some of them used abstract designs. Designs that represented a shaman's vision."

15 Suspicion

Wednesday morning I walked east along the dusty road toward Freddy's yard. In the distance I saw the shuffling form of Freddy in his checkered coat, his dark hat low over his ears. He made his way slowly in my direction.

"Nice to see you Freddy," I said as he approached. "You're out for a walk."

"I try."

"How are you feeling this morning?"

"Not so bad."

After his answer, there was a silence. We stood together near the low chain-link fence surrounding the elementary school. I said, "It's overcast this morning. Does that mean rain?"

"Perhaps." Another silence.

He looked into the distance, like a man preoccupied, but then he turned and we headed back toward his house.

"I brought you aspirin."

"Oh?" He looked up at me from under the brim of his hat. It was the first time he displayed any interest.

Arriving at his compound, we drew up chairs in the shade of the acacia, but we didn't sit down. I stood behind a chair and fished out the aspirin bottle from my pocket.

"I got these in America."

"Yes? That coming from America?" The tone of his voice seemed to imply that made it more potent. I felt like a charlatan.

Freddy's wife was nowhere in sight. Among the dishes and pans in the cooking area, clean dishes were laid out on a board. Several enameled cups were placed upside down in a row. Freddy selected one. He held the pill bottle, but his arthritic hands couldn't grasp the lid tightly enough to open it. After taking the bottle back from him, I unscrewed the lid and poured water from a plastic bottle into his cup. He threw two of the white pills into his mouth and washed them down with a loud gulp.

I stood near the base of a tree and found myself looking at his hat. The hat I had thought was brown felt yesterday, now looked to be suede. It was greasy with age and the nap was worn smooth. The repair I'd assumed had been done with packaging tape was actually a strip of tan-colored leather stitched around the top.

"What did you do for pain before you had aspirin?" I asked. I knew that he must have information on traditional cures for sore joints.

His answer puzzled me. "Razor blades. Ready to cutting. Then put the powder from burnt rope." Freddy took another gulp of water. I wasn't sure what he meant by "ready to cutting." The burnt rope was puzzling, as well. I formed a mental picture of some kind of vine used as either a rope or a remedy. I didn't pursue it.

I then asked him about the trance dance used by Bushmen for healing. Freddy looked away. He adjusted his hat and wiped his arm across his face, like he was wiping away perspiration. Then he began to talk again, continuing to answer my first question as if I hadn't asked another. "Some also that you drink, making a tea. Boil it. Watch it getting strong. You drink. I can't say the plant."

We walked back to the chairs in the middle of the yard. So far that morning, everything we talked about felt unfinished. I began to feel ill at ease.

"All the plants got a name. I don't know the English." Freddy eased himself into the ragged netting of his aluminum lawn chair. "Dr. Heinz was interested. We travel. Talk to Bushmens." I knew the name Dr. Heinz. I had run across a couple of books he had written about the Kalahari and Bushmen.

A little golden-furred dog appeared in the yard. He chewed on a stick for a few minutes and then took an interest in my foot. He began to gnaw on my sandal. I sat cross-legged, my left foot dangled about six inches above the sand where the puppy rolled over, lay on his back, and tried to sink his teeth into the sole of the shoe. I wiggled my foot to give him a challenge — my foot became a moving, struggling prey.

"Is this your hunting dog?" I asked.

"She's cheeky. Bite all the time," he chuckled.

The conversation had the feel of preliminaries; we were going through the exercise of becoming relaxed with each other again. I wanted to know more about Freddy's process of changing from one culture to another, but I was not sure we had the language. Yesterday, he had dodged the topic when I had asked him to tell me about his early experience with the Nharo.

I asked him about his sore knee and the spill he had taken on the horse.

"We were hunting. I was a young man. The horse fell in a hole," he said. The day before, he'd told me that it happened last year.

The puppy slobbered on my sandal before losing interest and wandering away. Across the yard, he found a cat about his size. Under the dishes, the two of them wrestled and growled, rolling in the dust.

"Do you know Dr. Heinz?" Freddy seemed to want to change the subject. Freddy assumed I knew Heinz. I knew that Heinz had done a study of herbal cures and that Freddy was one of his sources of information.

"No. I know about him. But we've never met."

"He stays in Maun now. Got a place there. His big son is there."

Heinz had written a memoir about his relationship with a Bushman woman named Namkwa, with whom he had a son. He came into the Kalahari initially as part of a medical research team doing a study of Bushmen in 1961, but quickly became a controversial figure. By his own description, in his early experiences he was insensitive to San culture. He disregarded essential relationships and created tension within the team through his clumsiness. In almost every story Heinz told about himself, his presence seemed to stimulate arguments and antagonisms.

But Freddy obviously enjoyed Heinz and talking about him seemed to restore his energy. At the time they worked together on medicinal herbs, Freddy must have been in his mid-sixties and Heinz about twenty years younger.

"Dr. Heinz is not coming here anymore. That German!" He said it as a familiar, friendly insult. "That one, he's all right; together we go to Namibia, all over Botswana . . . ." Freddy started to laugh, but his laughter turned into a coughing spell. "We go all that places." He spread his arms expansively.

I wondered if I could capitalize on Freddy's jovial mood. *Good things come from persistence*, I told myself. Yesterday, each attempt on my part to get him to talk about his life with the Nharo, growing up with Nharo childhood friends, came to an abrupt dead end. Maybe he hadn't understood what I was asking, but I was anxious to learn about the Nharo and thought I saw an opening.

"Freddy, you have lived with the Nharo for a long time. Your family is Nharo. You have traveled with them . . . worked with them . . .," I paused. I intended to continue and ask, "Could you tell me about your young Nharo friends and how you were influenced to move from one culture to another?"

In my mind everything I was saying led to an open-ended invitation for Freddy to reminisce about Nharo hunters, shooting game with the small reed arrows used by Bushman, collecting water in ostrich shell containers, tracking game in the desert.

But Freddy did not take it that way. Instead, he fixed me with a steady gaze and, for an instant, I saw fire in his eyes.

"I live with the Nharo, yes! I stay with them!" His voice was part trumpeting of elephant, part roaring of lion. There was something in the topic that brought up volatile emotions. He sounded exasperated and impatient. What I thought of as a gentle nudge to his memory became instead a lightning rod for his anger. His reaction caught me off guard.

"Yes, I stay with them!" he repeated. Freddy sounded exasperated as if I did not understand. I heard Freddy's anger and saw the flash of his eyes. For a split second, I felt the force of paternal displeasure sweeping over me like a strong wind. "I growing up with Nharos in Ghanzi. Dutch also. Young friends. All of them mixed with Nharos."

In those days a lot of his friends "mixed" with the Nharo, but Freddy was the only one I knew of who lived with them. He was also the only person of his generation still living. Was it the subject or was it my words? I rationalized that not everything about Freddy would show on the surface. Perhaps he did not remember, or did not place any importance on factual data such as dates, years — matters we Americans might consider vital statistics. As a result, some things will be unknowable for me.

Being on the receiving end of his anger made me squirm, but I found it curiously satisfying. I remembered how my father's eyes used to flash in the same way when he reproached me.

In some odd way I felt confirmed — Freddy acknowledged my existence.

This isn't to say, I didn't learn something. I did. I was beginning to get a picture of what was going on, though I couldn't quite put it into words yet.

Fortunately, Freddy's defensiveness was short-lived. Without additional prodding from me, he went back to reminiscing about early friends and hunting in Ghanzi.

"I stayed on a farm; we went hunting. We shoot springbok, duiker. Every Saturday we go get meat. In those days, ooooh, too much game. That time, as you sitting here, great many springbok. Too much." Freddy started coughing. When the coughing spell passed, he continued. "Government was mad to sell the game to other people. Selling elephant, buffalo. All the big game. Sell it to all the people. Huge fences were built." He referred to the veterinary fence that ended the big migrations in the Kalahari.

"Is there game now? Any at all?"

"Oh, yes, a few standing around in places. No more herds. Duikers, springbok. But in that time, everyday you can shoot meat. Every afternoon. Every afternoon. Anytime. Shoot two duiker. One duiker. If you want, shooting three and giving one to the boys."

Freddy seemed to be in a rant now. I could not follow everything he said, but I knew he was talking about something lost and the changes in the world he did not understand. In addition to his complaint about smaller herds and scarce game, he complained about the quality of *mealies*, the cornmeal porridge that accompanies every bite of food. The government was responsible.

"I can say that all of Ghanzi is farms. Now all the old Dutch are now going away from Ghanzi." Going away . . . he had used that earlier to describe the deaths of one of his wives and daughters.

Freddy paused. It was breakfast break time and the children dressed in their school uniforms waited in the yard. A three-legged pot sat over the coals of the fire. In it, the white porridge formed into fumaroles sending steam into the air. Freddy's wife ladled thick mealies onto the children's metal plates. The oldest girl filled several cups with milky tea. A small boy in short trousers poked at the sand with a stick. The puppy chased the stick, growling, and made the children laugh.

Freddy began telling me a story about a man named Mac MacIntyre. "He has two sons. I digging him wells." It was a long involved story. "Mac dies and people want to take the farm. The two sons ask me if I knowing Mac. I knowing him for years, working for him." He was describing an event from years earlier, but in the telling, distinctions between past and present were blurred. I had trouble following.

As Freddy began telling me about Mac MacIntyre, a Nharo man arrived in the yard. Other visitors had come by during the time I was there either to sit or to chat with Freddy. The new visitor pulled up a chair and sat next to Freddy. I guessed the man was thirty-ish. He wore a tan shop coat, and a wool pullover ski hat that sat bunched around the top of his head.

I lost track of Freddy's story and began to glance over at the activities of children across the yard and half-listen to the conversation. Among the confused details, I gathered that Freddy had to go to court. There was a lawsuit. A man owed Freddy 3,000 pula . . . or were the two MacIntyre sons trying to get back their father's farm? Somehow, Queen Elizabeth would vouch for Freddy's honesty.

"People are taking farms away. I am a witness; witness who knew father, can tell judge who owns farm. Magistrate talks to Queen Elizabeth . . . " Freddy rambled on about MacIntyre and began to now call him Boes . . . or maybe Bush . . . MacIntyre. "He died . . . I must go to Gaborone. I lost money and it's my fault."

As Freddy's story rambled, the man next to him leaned toward me in an aggressive posture. He sat no more than three feet away from me and fixed me with a stare. The man's complexion was Nharo, but his eyes were green. He removed his hat and clutched it in his hands. At that moment, he paid no more attention to Freddy than I did. His eyes glowered with curiosity and mistrust. In my two visits with Freddy, others had shown interest in me as a white-skinned person. I was used to that. But this man seemed openly suspicious.

Was Freddy's story pure fantasy? Or was there an element of fact — some unfinished business from the past? A gusting wind made hissing sounds in the acacias.

Suddenly — impertinently, I thought — the man turned and interrupted Freddy. Although he spoke in Nharo, his meaning was clear: Who is this white man sitting with you? They had a few words, and then the younger man turned to me and regarded me for half a minute before he spoke in Setswana.

"*Ke bidiwa*, Jim Morris," he spit out his introduction as if speaking in Setswana left a bad taste in his mouth.

"*Leina la me* John Ashford," I answered. We tried to make a stumbling conversation in Setswana. Where are you from? What is your business here? His questions were stated in a challenging way.

I answered as best I could. I was an American. I had been a teacher in the village of Tonota in the northeast of the country. He asked me a few more questions, but I couldn't understand his accent. Neither of us spoke enough Setswana to communicate.

In our brief exchange, however, it seemed to matter to Jim Morris that I was an American. That meant I was not a white South African. Once he understood that, he resettled himself in his chair and his posture became more relaxed and less aggressive.

Freddy took a faded blue bandanna from his pants pocket, removed his hat, and mopped his brow. Then he put the bandanna back and let his hat settle back around his ears.

"Jim works at the leather tannery," Freddy told me. "My father, James. My brother was Jim." My *brooder*, he said. "This one has my brother's name."

I guessed that Jim Morris must have done the repair on the crown of Freddy's greasy leather hat.

"You have a lot of Morrises living right here, around your house."

As I made the comment Freddy translated, and then Jim, the son, counted. He came up with twenty-four Morrises in this and the adjoining compounds.

"A large clan you have, Freddy."

Freddy laughed, "Yes, Morris, Morris."

Jim was clearly not interested in niceties or his father's paternal pride. He entered the conversation and wanted to say more. Again, he started speaking in Setswana, but very quickly I got lost. He switched to Nharo and Freddy translated.

Jim looked directly into my eyes as he spoke. He was talking about people who cannot have land. It was unfair that one group lived well while another group did not. When Bushmen children go to secondary school, they must travel all the way to Ghanzi and board away from home. They cannot live with their family.

"That's not right," he said, pausing to moisten his lips with his tongue. His eyes glistened with intensity.

"We cannot continue like this," Jim said. "The country belongs to everyone, but where is the land of the Bushman?" He listed the grievances of his people: jobs, economic development, education, land. Although I was the only person listening, he spoke with rhetorical calls to action as if he were addressing an audience at a political meeting.

"We have no land, unequal education. There needs to be a place for the Bushman — schools and land. We must fight it, mon. We must fight it."

A fire burned in Jim's eyes. Though he was speaking a language I had no knowledge of, the power in his voice made me sit up and pay attention. He could have gone on longer, but Freddy stopped mid-translation. He writhed out of the low aluminum frame chair and shuffled over to the barbed wire fence to pee in the sand.

Jim and I sat in silence and the pause gave me a minute to reflect on what I was seeing here. The picture of the two men seemed perfect to me. It was the picture of a younger man challenging his father. When the son came into the yard, he was clearly the man in charge. He was asserting his rights and questioning authority. The father translated the son's Nharo into English. The father was not the authoritarian figure who directed the fate of his family and offspring. He was the father, but he was also the white man. Although he had moved into the culture, he was also separate from it.

While Freddy peed, Jim fidgeted briefly, then rose from his chair and sauntered over to the board with the cups. He poured himself a cup of water and looked at me from a distance. By this time, Freddy had turned to walk back to his chair and I watched him shuffle across the sand. When my gaze returned to the place Jim had been standing, he was gone. Without a word or a wave, he disappeared from Freddy's yard.

16 The Scar

Freddy walked back across the yard in his careful, dignified steps. The sky, overcast earlier, was now a clear blue. The sun was almost directly overhead. Somewhere in the trees, doves called to one another and a brief gust of wind rustled sand and leaves.

As I waited for Freddy, I thought about the things we had talked about.

Yesterday, he'd told me about moving across the desert from one village to another. He had described the experience of hunting and killing a lion at the age of twelve, an incident that sounded to me like his initiation into manhood.

Today's conversation felt fragmented. Herbal cures, the disappearance of game, the problem with a man named MacIntyre. Nothing we'd talked about made sense. Freddy had seen so much and there had been so many changes in his lifetime.

But I was beginning to understand something.

He settled himself into the chair and took a couple of puffing breaths, "Mmph."

Was it my imagination? Freddy was beginning to look relaxed for the first time that morning. When he spoke, he looked directly into my eyes.

"You ask about hunting . . .," Freddy said. His comment was abrupt and I did not follow him at first. It was true, I had asked about that several times in various ways over the two days: *What can you tell me about the hunting in the old days? Did you live as a hunter? Did you hunt with bows? How did you hunt?* I'd hoped to learn whether he had hunted with Bushmen in the traditional way, but he had not answered my questions, no matter how I had phrased them. Instead, he'd become irritated. Now, he initiated the topic.

"Look . . . let me show you." Freddy took off his hat. Tilting his head to one side, he lifted his hair away from his ear to show me a scar. Then he traced a finger along the line that ran across the back of his head, from behind his right ear, under his hairline, and across the back of his head all the way to his other ear. It was an impressive scar.

I looked at the scar in wonder. "How did that happen?" I asked.

Freddy began to tell me about a day with his Nharo brother-in-law and another Bushman — good friends, working buddies. They had been repairing a fence and digging a new well near Kalkfontein for a farmer named Sharpe. They stopped in their work to hunt for meat. The men drove a ways in a wagon and then left the wagon and mule under a tree. Rains had been ample that year and everything was green. Water pooled and gurgled in a small sandy creek bed and the tall grass hissed against his trousers as Freddy walked with the men, who he called, "the boys." They thought they could find a duiker, one of the greyhound-size antelopes that grazed in the area. Freddy had brought along a twenty-two gauge rifle for the purpose. But it was not long before the three mongrel dogs with them began making too much noise. With the moaning and groaning of those damn dogs, any antelope in the area would be out of range in no time.

Freddy was complaining to his brother-in-law about the dogs when the other Bushman picked up a track.

"He see the spoor," Freddy said. "It's a big leopard. Then we see the leopard under a tree. When he hear us he running away. My brother-in-law say, 'We must track his spoor' and I say, 'We have only a point-two-two.' "

But a leopard was a hazard in the area. They had to get him.

"We going after leopard. We follow and we follow." The dogs bayed and cried. Freddy could tell that the dogs were scared. "I tell the other people, 'These dogs are frighting for the leopard.' We got three dogs. The people say no, 'These dogs killing leopards before.' Alright, we went after him. But we lose him in the grass and he get away. We follow, then we get him up in a tree. He's trapped and the dogs won't chase. So the leopard knows now the dogs are afraid. He comes right at us. Dogs run away, other people run into the grass. They all run."

Freddy mopped his brow again with his blue bandana.

"I stand here looking and I see that leopard coming for me. What can I do? I can't run away. He would got me nice. He would got me from the back if I run. So, I stand. He come. Jumping up me."

Freddy lifts his hat and shows me with his fingers like teeth over the back of his head. "He take me here and I take him on his throat. And I put him down. I shoot him with the point-two-two. I shoot him nice. He jump up and go a few steps then lies there in the grass. And he lay there and the blood. Ooh. I could not open my eyes. Only hearing the blood. Throbbing noise. It take a long time for stop the blood. I telling the people, 'Take the rope. Put me in the water. Put the rope on the wound, wash it out. Wet rope and pressure. Then we see the blood stop.' "

"With a twenty-two rifle, your shot has to be good," I said. "Perfect."

Freddy made a noise that sounded like he was clearing his throat — disgust. "It's not a gun. You can kill small animals. Duiker. Good for birds. Bird gun."

I remembered his earlier story about the lion and how he had put the rifle in the lion's mouth to release his friend from its grip. As a lad of twelve, he hadn't backed down from the lion. And even with his head in the leopard's mouth, he was able to accurately shoot the predator with a small-gauge rifle.

For a few minutes we chatted about the Nharo hunting with poisoned tipped arrows, cures for snake bite, and other miscellaneous subjects, but I knew my time with Freddy was coming to a close for now.

The reason was very mundane: Gen and I were running out of groceries. We had not intended to stay in Dkar when we left Maun. We had to go to Ghanzi to resupply. It was very likely that we'd return.

Listening to Freddy talk about his life had taken me into another era — a time before roads, when goods and people traveled by wagons pulled by oxen or mules and when huge areas of the country were ruled by chiefs who were as powerful as kings. But tomorrow I would leave Dkar. Already I was beginning to miss this old man and our conversations.

I began to realize that the many visitors who'd shown up during the two days I'd spent with Freddy were not just coming to see him. They undoubtedly wanted to know what Freddy was talking about with me. Were these two white men talking about Nharo people with the racist words that whites sometimes use?

I had created an uncomfortable situation for Freddy. My idealization of the man and his life was out of proportion in the same way as my earlier idealization of the San culture. And in my attempt to sort out the reality from the fantasy, I had asked the wrong questions.

Freddy for his part, stayed away from those subjects that he knew might cause offense. I came seeking a romantic myth of a white man who became a Bushman. What I wanted him to talk about was precisely what he wanted to avoid. When I asked him to tell me about growing up with the Nharo, I was pursuing a romantic myth — perhaps a racist myth. He knew more about that than I did.

Before I left Freddy's yard, I told him I was going to Ghanzi. I hoped to return to see him another day, perhaps next week.

"In Ghanzi, is there someone else I can talk to about the Nharo? The Bushmen?"

"See John Hardbattle. His farm is in Chapango. Ask John. Young people have papers, can write Nharo. They can tell you 'what say this, what say this.'"

I rose from my seat, gave Freddy a wave, and said, "Goodbye. Hope to see you in a few days." Then I walked slowly back to the hostel.

I had enjoyed sitting with Freddy. Being in his presence filled me with optimism and the visit had cleared away many of my doubts. Our trip here was not just a meaningless obsession. During the hours we'd sat in his yard, I'd learned something.

17 Pieces of a Puzzle

After talking to Freddy for two days, what did I know?

I knew very little about his inner life, but I had recorded the history and the social dynamics of the community in my notes. For some of the details I used my imagination and perhaps a dose of longing.

Freddy's fragmented stories enabled me to fill in gaps about places where we had camped — Nata, Nxai Pan, and Maun. Using historical information, as well as stories and data gathered by sociologists in Ghanzi, I tried to piece together a picture of the early life of this man who crossed from one culture to another.

Within the context of Freddy's white community, it seemed like it might be an act of rebellion or disobedience for him to suddenly declare that he was taking a Bushman wife. But was it really a sudden turn about? Or had his upbringing made this a perfectly natural step?

Freddy had told me he was from the village of Serowe, which was located in the Central District, south of Francistown, along the eastern edge of the desert. In the early part of the century, Serowe was the village of a king,

Khama III, or Khama the Good, one of the great African leaders of his time. Khama had been educated by the British and got along well with Europeans. He enjoyed being around teachers, thus it is reasonable to assume that Freddy's father, James Morris, a teacher in Serowe, knew Khama.

In fact, James Morris probably had an audience with the king when he decided to leave the village. At that time, the comings and goings in traditional villages usually involved an audience with the chief as a matter of etiquette. Morris would have told the chief of his plan to move to the Okavango, and it was likely Khama gave him references and contacts among the Batawana.

Morris would then have loaded his family and their belongings into a wagon to make the 300-mile trip across the sands of the Kalahari Thirstland from Serowe to Maun.

Typical transport in those days was a relatively light wagon pulled by a span of twelve oxen. The split hooves of the oxen gave them an advantage over other animals, such as horses or mules, walking in the shifting surface of desert sand. The twelve oxen were yoked under a straight piece of wood laid across their shoulders just behind the humped neck. Each animal was then fixed inside a collar with a leather strap. The weight of the load was evenly distributed among the huge animals when together they pushed against their collars. On a good day, they could travel at a speed of two miles per hour.

Iron pots and pans, kettles and pails, and shovels and picks hung from rings underneath the wagon. As the large wheels of the wagon rolled over the sand, the bumps and dips caused a clatter of noise. Hanging from the back of the wagon, chained to the platform and with one end fastened to the axletree, was a baggage compartment called a trap. The trap contained bags of corn and chaff — plain wheat straw — which the animals ate mixed with mealies when there was nothing to graze.

A tin box containing the family's supply of utensils, blankets, bundles of clothing, and various other goods, including, perhaps, a saddle would have been on the platform. Freddy's infant crib would have ridden in the wagon on one of the seats. Inside the wagon on the platform between the seats, the family's more valuable possessions — a drug chest, and guns and ammunition — would be kept.

The family would be living on what they could hunt and gather until farming could begin, so they needed a good supply of ammunition. A box of cartridges containing 8,000 rounds was heavy, but it would provide for a year's hunting and enough extra to sell or trade for other needs.

Once the Morris family arrived in their new surroundings, they would have found a life much more dependent on African tribes-people for help. According to Freddy, James Morris made friends with the Africans and accepted the people he met. He was a good businessman. He knew the language and more than likely was good-naturedly tolerant of different customs.

In his new capacity as a trader, James Morris traveled.

Freddy had said, "My father coming and going to village near rivers, other side of Maun — Boro River, Thamalekalane River — Kurube was the village. My father coming to Kurube. Stay a time there. Then he going away to Masire. There he buy a shop. Yes."

Morris carried cattle and goods south *onderaf* — down yonder, to South Africa — and brought back commodities to trade. While he moved between cultures and over distances, his family lived in isolation. Willem Abraham De Klerk, in his book, *The Puritans in Africa*, used the phrase "idyllic isolation" to describe the way of life of white settlers — "people who got lost in Africa." Farms were spread over a vast area, but were self-sufficient with fruit from the trees and crops produced by the arable land. In Freddy's description, game came to their doorstep.

When a family moved from a large village to an isolated farm, the wife had by far the greater burdens in the change. She still had to be a mother, run the household, milk and feed the animals, and work in the garden that provided much of the food. In order to accomplish it all, much of the care of the children had to be turned over to an African woman. From her, the children received their early education and learned a culture and language altogether different from that of their parents. Freddy grew up in this world from the time he was weaned. His teachers, surrogate mothers, and playmates were outside the Calvinist traditions of most of the white settlers.

"So we are staying there. I growing, getting to be a man now. Running around . . .," Freddy laughed as he spoke. He didn't explain what he meant by, "Running around." I could only guess why he laughed and why he did not explain.

"Later, my father sold the shop and butchery. We leave Masire. Old Captain Machibe, lives there, Batawana chief. They were good friends. Machibe then going away to Maun. My father tell him, 'Yes, you throw me away and you go away. So now I'm also going away to farm.' Then he come from there, from Masire to Tsau. So, we are staying in Tsau. Later, my father coming from Tsau to Ghanzi."

Eventually, Freddy's father became a very rich man, reputed to own as many as 900 cattle after the family's move to Ghanzi. He continued to travel, taking goods from Ghanzi — cattle, hides, ostrich plumes, ivory, and *biltong* (jerky) — to South Africa, and returning with food, ammunition, fabric, and other goods special ordered for patrons. Freddy, who held his father in awe, cared for the cattle and worked around the farm.

In Africa, killing a lion is usually considered one's passage into manhood. Freddy had killed his first lion at the age twelve — and he would kill several more in his life — but he had a greater test in his future. Freddy would have to face his father and his community. Killing a lion was minor by comparison.

Freddy's father was a Scotsman who had come to Africa to fight in the Boer War. In Serowe, he met and married a round-faced woman of Dutch heritage. She was stocky and strong, raised in the protectorate near Mafeking. She exuded pioneer toughness. All her life her family had trekked and led a pioneer existence. She knew what it took to move from place to place in the desert and what it took to be the wife of a merchant. She could handle herself on a farm where the chores were numerous and the work difficult.

The traditions of the Dutch Boers were frontier, rural, and isolated. A self-sufficient, strictly Calvinist people who were strongly individualistic and Protestant, there was not much to bind them as a national group until the British tried to impose their English sense of order. Increasingly, the Boers referred to themselves as Afrikaners, just as the version of the Dutch language they spoke was beginning to be known as Afrikaans.

Freddy's mother was a Taljaard, a Dutch family that settled in South Africa in the seventeenth century. At the turn of the twentieth century, after their loss in the Boer war, the Dutch intensified their resentment toward the English. There was intermarriage between Dutch and English, but attitudes dictated the relationship in the home. For instance, Freddy's mother was bilingual, but as a sign of her Afrikaner solidarity all of her conversations with her husband were in Dutch. That became Freddy's first language as well. When he grew old enough to work with his father, he learned English. He also learned other languages in order to function in the complex society he lived in.

Besides the linguistic conventions followed by the family, there was the cultural environment of the Afrikaner. When Freddy's family moved to Ghanzi, Bushmen and Afrikaners lived side by side. Bushmen still lived a nomadic style of life, but there was an exchange of skill, technology, and protection in those days. The whites were extremely poor and learned about veld food from their association with Bushmen. Living near whites, the Bushmen gained protection from the slave raids of northern tribal groups and had access to a stable source of water and milk. During years of drought, Bushmen and Afrikaners gathered tsama melons and hunted together. Afrikaner settlers recognized that the land was occupied and mapped by the indigenous people. Afrikaners accepted the Bushman place names and used them on their farms. "Ghanzi" itself is a word in one of the Bushman languages.

In the Ghanzi region, the two groups lived together on the same farms for years with Bushman bands coming and going as weather, seasons, and game dictated, and Freddy came of age in that society of Afrikaners.

However, the society that evolved between the whites and Bushmen was one in which the groups were on a familiar but unequal basis. Bushmen were gradually pushed off their land on the Ghanzi Ridge and, due to the superior water technology of whites, became more dependent on the colonialists. They were two peoples undergoing "separate development," a euphemistic expression for apartheid. Eventually, the commercialization of cattle grazing transformed the entire region and undercut the hunting and gathering way of life of the Bushman.

Socially, however, the groups were more intimate the longer they shared the same territory. Among Afrikaner men, there was the expectation of sexual adventures with Bushman women, just as Victorian men in other circumstances visited prostitutes. As a result, there are many green-eyed Bushmen in the Ghanzi area. A word in Afrikaans, *rondlopers*, is used in the Ghanzi District to describe men who walk about, with the implication that they carry on, or have sexual liaisons, with Bushman women. A study by a pair of sociologists in the 1970s claimed that nearly all Afrikaner men maintained concubines, though in public they maintained strict adherence to Afrikaner attitudes. For example, a white man might secretly keep a Bushman mistress. However, among other whites he uttered the expected racial comments — he will curse his workers as unreliable or express frustration about their Stone Age life style.

In 1973, the same sociologists reported that they knew of only one white man in the Ghanzi area who lived with his Bushman wife. With their three children, they moved wherever there was work. The man owned cattle that grazed on a farmer's land, and he supported his family by building fences, digging wells, and contracting for labor. The sociologists did not name the man, but they included a photograph. Their book was where I first saw the picture of Freddy Morris with his fourth Nharo wife and three children.

Late Wednesday afternoon, after I'd returned from my second trip to Freddy's compound, Gen and I sat in the shaded doorway of the hostel. It was too hot to move. I leaned my bucket stool back against the log wall.

"How's it going with Freddy?" Gen asked.

"I enjoy hearing him talk."

"You said you wanted to learn his story. Did it happen?"

"Slowly, but surely. Lots of gaps."

"Is that frustrating for you?"

"No, it's not frustrating. I can't expect everything on a silver platter. But Freddy mentioned that a man named John Hardbattle who lives in Ghanzi may be able to fill in some details."

"Know anything about him?"

"Other people have told me about him. He's part Nharo and knows a lot about the history of the area. Freddy told me that Hardbattle's father was Scottish, and along with Freddy's father they were the only two Scots in Ghanzi. I think Hardbattle might be a good person to meet."

"So you're going to keep trying then, to learn Freddy's story?"

"I want to learn about the Nharo. I'm not sure how much John Hardbattle knows about Freddy. But as far as Freddy's story goes, I'm fascinated by it."

"Fascinated? Seems more like obsessed." There was a long pause before Gen continued. "You've put in a lot of effort. Besides your research in the library, we've driven 1,300 kilometers — that's about 800 miles, I think — from Francistown across the desert. Plus your conversations with him."

Another long pause.

"Did *you* ever hear *your* father talk about his life?"

"I was too young."

"You lived with him for fifteen years."

"He never talked about growing up. Seems funny now. As a child, it didn't even occur to me that he might have had a childhood." I laughed.

"And you didn't know him as an adult, when you were old enough to ask."

"Right. That's something I've missed."

Gen's eyes sparkled as if there was a joke that had somehow passed me by. "Remember when you first told me about Freddy? You had read a story about him in a newspaper."

I nodded.

"Do you remember how you became so defensive when I mentioned something about your father?"

I smiled.

"That's it, though, isn't it?" she said.

"But even with my defensiveness, I was aware of parallel journeys."

It was Gen's turn to be puzzled. "What do you mean?"

"Just thinking about that conversation. I told you about Freddy . . . .. I wanted to meet him. But there were a lot of other things I wanted to learn, as well. I just didn't know what they all were."

"Hmm," Gen smiled. "Parallel journeys. You travel across the desert. You piece together fragments of an old man's life story . . . .." She began to laugh. "Then, whose story is it?"

18 The Garden

We left Dkar late Friday morning under an overcast sky to begin the short drive to Ghanzi. The clouds burned off while we bounced along a wide sandy road, and by the time we reached the small town it felt as if we were driving into an oven.

Freddy had told me that John Hardbattle's farm was in Chapango. I had never heard of the place, but I was sure we'd be able to get directions in Ghanzi.

Ghanzi was a remote government station with standard government-issue housing — concrete block, corrugated metal roof, and two bedrooms. These were houses for people who were paid to live here. One cluster of homes was painted white with blue trim, another cluster painted yellow. Small white rondevaals housed lower-paid government officers. For most of the residents, Ghanzi was a two-year mandatory posting to work at the utility, prison, secondary school, post office, or police station.

I'd heard that the Kalahari Arms Hotel provided a tenting spot on a green triangle of lawn in the back. Gen and I stopped to buy groceries and then headed to the hotel. We set up our tent and dozed on our sleeping bags for thirty minutes. In the afternoon, we sipped cold soda under an umbrella near the swimming pool. Gen sketched for a while and then swam in the kidney-shaped pool. I updated my notes and read through the news clippings I'd been collecting.

Late in the afternoon, the weather began to play tricks. Clouds gathered and wind threatened to blow my writing tablet off the table. The yellow pages of my pad rippled as I did my best to hold the paper down and while I held the pages, my hat nearly blew away. Overhead the clouds grew darker. Lightning flashed in the distance and thunder rattled faintly.

There was no point in my trying to work, so I checked our tent stakes, zipped the openings, and adjusted the rain fly to make sure we'd have a dry place in the event of a storm. I planned to look for John Hardbattle's farm the next day, but since we still had two hours of daylight we decided to drive around and get our bearings.

Near the truck I met a small man with all the facial features of a Bushman; he was looking for handouts. He wore a dark suit jacket and a drooping fedora.

"*Motsoko*," he said. "*Ke kopa motsoko.*" Cigarette. I'd like a cigarette.

"Ehe, dumela." Yes, I answered.

Gen was in the truck by this time and the passenger door was open. I reached across her to grab a package of cigarettes and matches from the glove compartment. As an ex-smoker, I carried tobacco only for handouts. I shook the pack and the man took a cigarette. I lit it for him and he walked off.

Almost a mile east of the hotel, the unpaved main road ended near the Itekeng Secondary School and the dormitory building. Seeing the dormitory reminded me of Jim Morris's complaint about Bushman children having to live away from home.

A U-turn took us past police barracks, and then warehouses and offices for the Telecommunications Ministry that operated the microwave and telephone service. The edge of town looked out on a squatter community, a sprawling slum of traditional housing and corrugated metal shacks. From there, the road headed west straight across the desert. A group of a dozen people waited at the side of the road hoping for a ride to either Kalkfontein or Mamuno near the Namibian border. People in the group waved and looked expectantly at the truck. I made a circular motion with my downward pointed index finger — like stirring water with my finger — to tell them I couldn't give anyone a ride. *Just driving around.*

By continuing west on the road, I was sure we could eventually arrive at John Hardbattle's ranch. But it was time to get back. At a wide spot, I slowed the truck to turn and head toward the hotel, but a hundred feet before we reached the hotel, I spotted a sign I'd missed earlier, "Ghanzi Crafts." In Gaborone, my friends Tim and Esther has told me that a John Hardbattle served some function with Ghanzi Crafts.

The store did not appear to be open, but a red bakkie sat parked next to the gate in front. I thought perhaps someone here could give me directions to John Hardbattle's place. I parked behind the bakkie and walked to the chain-link fence. The gate was padlocked, but a door into the building stood ajar and a man leaned in the shadows. I waved to get his attention.

"Yes," he said, "how are you?"

"Hello, can you tell me how I can find a man named John Hardbattle?"

"I'm John Hardbattle."

What luck!

Hardbattle had been a shadowy figure in my awareness since my conversation with Tim and Esther. They'd described him as an activist for the Bushmen. Then Freddy mentioned him yesterday. Now he stood just thirty feet away. However, I couldn't see his face.

"Look, I can't talk to you now," he said. "I'm waiting for a phone call."

A truck passed in the sand behind me creating dust and noise. Hardbattle's words were nearly drowned out.

"Meet me at the hotel," he called.

Conversation was impossible. I gave him a thumbs up.

"Garden Bar." He was shouting now, "In back."

The Garden Bar, like the hotel itself, seemed perched precariously on the edge of the desert. Squares of sod had been laid to create a grass-carpeted patio. Desert sand began at the exact point where the carpet ended.

Gen and I ordered juice. Peach for her, grape for me. She wore her swimsuit under an open shirt and a wrap-around denim skirt.

"I'd like to meet him," she said. "Then I'll go back to the pool. That'll give you a chance to get acquainted. Maybe you and I can have a late dinner."

The waitress had a long walk between the bar inside the hotel and the patio and she didn't seem to be in much of a hurry. I had time to observe that someone had made an effort to decorate the Garden Bar. The main feature was a display of water cascading into a shallow tub lined with pebbles. From the tub, a clear vinyl tube took water into a plastic fountain. The fountain sprayed three feet into the air and the water was then pumped back. A heavy-duty orange extension cord passed under tables and chairs across the grass to the pump. A fig tree grew at one end of the display.

In about five minutes, the waitress returned carrying two cartons of Fruit Tree juice. Straws floated up from the top of each carton.

I had just taken the first sip through the straw when a small white dog with orange and black spots wandered toward our table. The dog gave the impression of suffering terribly from the heat — every movement seemed like torture, his expression extremely pitiful — I felt immediate affection for the poor animal. He stopped a few feet away to observe us for a minute before shuffling under our table and curling up in the grass by my feet. Within minutes, his weight gradually settled on my sandals and I felt the warmth of his fur.

Forty five minutes later, a red bakkie pulled into the parking lot, the same mini-truck I'd seen earlier in front of Ghanzi Crafts. A tall neatly dressed man emerged. He spotted me, waved, and headed toward the table where Gen and I sat.

Hardbattle wore carefully pressed casual clothing, a short-sleeved maroon shirt, and charcoal slacks. He looked to be fortyish, had dark curly hair, a thin black mustache, and light skin. John Hardbattle would be a difficult man to fix in a place or a continent if a person knew nothing about his background. In North America he might be described as looking Hispanic, but I also saw Nharo traits in his face and his eyes were slightly almond shaped. When we introduced ourselves, I noticed his British accent. The accent added further to the puzzle of the man.

The waitress stood near the bar. I gave her a high sign. Gen excused herself. "Back a little later," she said and waved.

Hardbattle pulled a vinyl chair from under the table and settled in. He hadn't noticed the resting dog. Reluctantly, the dog got to his feet and moved five feet away to a patch of sand where he scraped out a shallow hole and snuggled in.

"Where are you from in North America?" Hardbattle asked.

"Seattle."

For a second, he furrowed his brow. "Mmm . . . hmm. Don't know much about the place. Airplanes come from there, right?"

I nodded.

"I seem to remember," he said, "a great chief. Chief Seattle. I have heard of him."

The waitress brought a menu when she arrived and stood by our table, but Hardbattle didn't need a menu. "Rock shandy and an omelet," he told her.

I said nothing, but wondered, *What's a rock shandy?* I ordered a juice.

As soon as the waitress turned toward the bar, Hardbattle folded his hands on the table and announced, "I'll talk to you, but I have some conditions." From the tone of his voice, it was clear he was granting a concession. He said it as if this was the ordinary way to start a conversation. "I don't want our conversation to be taped and I won't talk about my personal life." His British accent lent a sense of authority to his words.

"Sure." What else could I say? I wanted to talk to the man, but the way this was starting out jarred me. It felt like interview jiujitsu and I was already on the mat.

"I spent a couple of days in Dkar and talked with Freddy Morris," I told him, hoping that mention of Freddy would establish a level of trust. "I'm interested in background on Ghanzi and anything you can tell me about the Bushmen in the area. I've been told you're the man to talk to."

The waitress reappeared with two drinks. Hardbattle's rock shandy was a reddish drink in a tall tapered glass. A single ice cube floated in the mysterious liquid. My juice was served in the same kind of carton as before, a straw punched through a hole in the top.

"I can tell you about Ghanzi, sure. And the people." He took a sip of his drink, leaned back, and threw his arm over the back of the chair. His relaxed posture made me think he wanted a fresh start. After a taking a moment to catch his breath, he said, "I know it sounds abrupt, but I don't mean it that way." Hardbattle paused. "I do need to make a distinction between my private life and my public roles. I didn't mean to say I wouldn't talk about myself." He set the glass on the surface of the table and, for a minute, played with the moisture on the outside. "It's just that I won't talk about my family or people close to me. We have to have that understood."

His words softened the atmosphere a little, which I appreciated. I'd begun to wonder what this was about. I didn't know enough about him to ask intimate questions.

"I know everyone here and everyone knows me. I'm a farmer, a rancher, a cattleman. But most of my time these days is spent working on behalf of the Bushman cause. The term I like to use is "First People of the Kalahari."

"Currently, I'm in the process of organizing the First People of the Kalahari Foundation. Ghanzi Crafts will be the headquarters. I funded that business and now I serve on the board. I started it so there'd be a place for Bushmen to sell crafts for cash. Cash economy is something none of the Bushmen groups have ever had. In the modern world, cash is power. So making money is a start for people. People bring handicrafts into the store and we sell them. The craftsmen and women get ninety percent. No one else would do that for them. In the city, crafts are sold for many times what the craftspeople are paid. You buy an artifact from Ghanzi Crafts, and the money goes to the person who created it."

His explanation was done in a businesslike manner, in a tone of voice like that of a promoter. To me, it seemed natural that he'd be advocating the cause of the Bushmen and the foundation he'd established.

He sipped his drink and shifted. "The foundation, First People of the Kalahari, is intended to serve the social cause of the indigenous people. The Bushmen were here before anyone else thought of coming and I think it's important to keep reminding the powers that be of that fact."

Intent on listening, I was suddenly aware of the waitress approaching us with a platter in her hand.

"This place was different when I was born. There have been a lot of changes." His tone shifted when he began talking about the past. "My mother was half Nharo, my father Scottish. He settled in Ghanzi early in the century, about the same time as Freddy Morris's father arrived. I was raised as a Nharo child, slept in a hut, hunted small game, played bows and arrows with my friends. I attended mission schools.

"Later on, my father sent me to Hull in Yorkshire for my education. He had some family there. So, I lived overseas for several years and studied in England. Eventually, I inherited the ranch from my father."

The waitress set down the oval plate, but Hardbattle did not seem to notice. The steaming omelet was huge and included a pile of French fries. The waitress laid out a napkin and utensils.

Conversation stopped for a minute while he leaned in and began to eat. He held his fork in his left hand, upside down, and pushed food with the knife onto the fork. "So, maybe we can start with Ghanzi. Some background first, history." He chewed as he spoke and then washed the food down with his drink. "Have you heard of the Dorsland Trekkers?"

I nodded my head. I'd heard of them, but didn't know much. Only that Freddy's grandparents had been part of that trek.

"They were the first group of whites to move here. Dorsland, or Thirstland, Trekkers. The first wave from South Africa consisted of religious zealots convinced that Beulah Land was out here and God had set aside the land to be ruled by white South Africans. They had a disastrous migration across the Kalahari. Half of the people died en route and most of their livestock was gone by the time they got here."

Hardbattle spoke calmly, as if he were telling his own story, or the story of his own people. *How could Hardbattle speak without derision or resentment?* I wondered. A silence followed. For a moment, I listened to the gurgle of water in the fountain and quiet hum of the electric pump.

Hardbattle finished his rock shandy. His empty glass and plate sat before him on the table. The waitress was close at hand, and he gave her a wave. "Fill my glass, please. The same."

"And a shandy for me," I said. I wanted to say the word and satisfy my curiosity. After a slight pause, Hardbattle furrowed his brow and remembered where he was in his story.

"The trekkers who came in the nineteenth century settled here for a short time, but found the conditions too harsh. Dirt poor for years, they couldn't make a living. The Nharo helped them find veld food, but eventually most of the trekkers left to push on into Namibia or Angola. At that time another person became important in their history," he said. "A man named Worthington. Worthington was a doctor, a natural born leader. But he was colored and it was ironic, that when they got here they picked a colored man as their leader."

The term "colored," was a legal designation in South Africa for a person of mixed race and a term used in Botswana. The mention of Worthington seemed to provide a punctuation mark. Hardbattle's arm had been over the chair back, now he leaned forward and stretched his arms.

In that moment, I had a glimmer of insight into what he was telling me. The stories of the Afrikaners, the British, and the Nharo in Ghanzi were all part of Hardbattle's story. Hardbattle belonged to all sides. That was why he could relate this background for me without defensiveness.

"The Afrikaners, the Dutch-speaking whites who stayed, lived together on the farms with Bushmen. Bushmen benefited from the technology of the whites, who had the means to obtain water. By the same token, whites were extremely poor and with the help of the Bushmen, they learned about food in the veld. During years of drought, Bushmen and Afrikaners joined together to gather food, and to hunt. But the trekkers who remained here were in a sorry state. They were classed at the bottom of the social ladder, as a kind of blight. British administrators lumped Afrikaners and Nharo together in a position of equality. They were equally miserable.

"Whites survived only because the Nharo helped them. Afrikaners of that generation owed a big debt to the Bushmen for their survival. Of course, their children forgot the debt. The next generation began fencing their farms and viewed the Nharo as squatters on private property. When the farms were fenced they no longer needed help keeping herds together and the idea of sending the Bushmen off to settlements began to take hold.

"Botswana became independent in 1966 and, almost immediately, beef prices rose. Farmers became wealthy and powerful, while the Bushmen were relegated to squatter status. The farmers here have profited from an international market for beef. Dirt poor for years, then suddenly they became rich. As a result of an agreement, European countries pay better than market prices. We receive a subsidy that sends money to the farmers. Like me. The agreement was a windfall for farmers. They basically got rich by doing nothing. Just by sitting on the land."

The waitress returned and placed two glasses on our table. Hardbattle's drink looked the same as before, a red drink in a tall glass with a cube of ice. I'd expected the same. After all, I ordered a shandy. But my drink was honey-colored with no ice.

What gives? I didn't know what the contents were in his glass, but it must have had a good shot of grenadine. That was the red part.

I took a sip. The drink was cold and I could feel the carbonation on my tongue. At first it tasted like beer. The next sip tasted like ginger ale. I should have asked Hardbattle, but I couldn't bring myself to say anything. I felt like a hick. After my second sip, the combination of beer and ginger ale tasted cloyingly sweet, and my shandy sat nearly untouched.

We talked for an hour while people began arriving for dinner. Couples and small groups made their way across the grass. Some went into the hotel restaurant, while others took tables outside in the garden.

A tall blond man and his wife walked past our table on their way to the indoor restaurant. The man recognized Hardbattle and reached out to shake his hand. "Say, congratulations, John. Mother and child are doing fine, I trust."

150

John Hardbattle shifted nervously and smiled. "Yes. Fine. As well as could be expected." His voice was controlled and his manners impeccable. "They've received good care." He chatted with the man, greeted the wife, and after a minute or two the couple walked on.

"First child?" I asked.

"Yes."

"When was the baby born?"

"January sixteenth." That was about a month earlier.

"A change in your lifestyle, then?"

"Actually, no. Mother and child are 10,000 miles away. When I saw you, I was trying to make a phone call to Norway to talk to my fiancé."

His discomfort was obvious. I could tell he hadn't wanted to say as much as he did. But it was enough to remind me of something I'd heard about "an activist and his fiancé." In Gaborone, Tim and Esther had told me about an activist who had gotten under the skin of officials in the government. Seeking to retaliate, they'd deported his Norwegian fiancé. Until that moment, I hadn't realized that Hardbattle was "the activist."

I repeated to him what Tim and Esther had said.

"There's more to it than that," he responded and then became silent for a minute. "Yes," he said, finally. "Things have happened because of my activities."

At that moment, Gen rejoined us. She pulled a chair away from the table and sat down. In the awkward silence that followed, she seemed to be aware it was a ticklish time to interrupt.

We talked for almost two more hours, and I lost track of time. When I looked over to where the dog had settled, I saw that he'd left. Blackness was settling in. Ragged clouds covered most of the sky and the air had turned chilly. A half-moon winked through gaps in the racing clouds overhead. Wind gusted around the table.

"How have the rains in Ghanzi been this year?" I asked.

"We haven't had rain now for two years," Hardbattle said. "It's building up to rain now, I hope."

A string of light bulbs had been turned on to create a festive atmosphere in the patio. The wires looped casually from the hotel through the branches of the fig tree and cast a dim light that was mostly absorbed by the blackness.

"When's the rain going to come, do you think?"

"It should be raining right now," Hardbattle laughed. "Actually, it's the wind. It seems to carry the clouds away. We'll see. There's still a chance we'll get rain."

"People in Dkar told me it was raining quite heavily the other day over near the border, to the west."

"Yes, near the Ghanzi Ridge. It's quite a high plateau. But if the winds are too strong, the clouds go right overhead."

In the near darkness, we stood up to say goodbye and Hardbattle invited us to come out to his farm the next day. "Come in the afternoon, I have business to take care of in the morning. Stay the night and we can talk some more tomorrow and the next day."

"Do I need any special directions?"

"No. Just drive west. You'll see the sign, 'Jackalspits.'"

19 Jackalspits

It was hot and clear the next day, but by afternoon the sky turned dark again. Clouds seemed ready to burst when Gen and I drove west along the main road to Hardbattle's place. When we reached the sign that said "Jackalspits," I turned left. Above us, on a slight rise, was a stand of shade trees waving in the wind. I assumed the house would be among the trees. When our tires rattled noisily over the cattle guard, it occurred to me that we had just rung the doorbell.

I parked in the drive near an arbor of flowering vines. Pink bougainvillea spilled over a paved walk and we were greeted by a stout, brindle dog. The dog bared his teeth and flattened his ears, wagging his tail vigorously. When I patted him on the neck, he leaned forcefully into my shin so that I couldn't walk until I petted him some more.

The dog and I were at an impasse when I was rescued by a Nharo woman who appeared from behind the house. Her head was wrapped in a dark-blue scarf and she had a gray sarong around her waist. "John return soon," she said in a quiet voice. "I bring tea."

She motioned us to a patio table near the arbor, and ten minutes later she brought a tray to our table with cups and saucers, a sugar bowl, two small spoons, and a pitcher of scalded goat milk. In the center of the tray was a French Press pot with dark, loose-leaf tea floating on the surface. There must have been some uncertainty in my mind about Hardbattle's invitation because I found the tea service reassuring. He did expect us, even though he was not home.

From the arbor we looked across a lawn toward a tile-roofed ranch house. Grape vines grew heavily on a trellis and cattle lowed in the distance. The smell of cattle manure hung in the air.

Thirty minutes passed, we had finished our tea.

"John did say he had business in the morning," I said. "Must've been more business than he thought."

"We're way too early," Gen said. "I heard him say, 'Come at four.' "

"No, I'm sure he said, 'Come over in the afternoon.'" My watch said two-thirty.

"He said four."

Gen sat in a plastic lawn chair with her shoulder bag near her feet. Her bag held her sketch pad, her knitting, and a half-read Michener novel about South Africa. If we had to wait a while, she had plenty to entertain herself with.

I felt agitated and wandered over to the truck to get a book of short stories by Bessie Head. For two hours I read and strolled around the yard. The weather kept changing. A solid bank of clouds formed a wall in the west, but wind tore at the edges to reveal patches of blue sky.

Across from the table where we'd had tea was a shop building holding several trucks and tractors in open bays. Each bay contained specialized mechanical, diagnostic, or welding equipment. I walked over to get a closer look. Inside one bay sat a tractor with the engine removed. In another, tires of different sizes were stacked for repair. Testing equipment with various gauges lined the wall of another bay. The amount of equipment and investment was impressive. The shop included everything a rancher needed for maintenance on work vehicles.

I had walked past the repair bays several times before I noticed that a thick layer of dust had accumulated on everything inside. It appeared that work had stopped some time ago.

To the north of the shop, hulks of several 1970s-era Jeep Wagoneers cluttered an overgrown corner of the yard. A fender was missing here, a door there. But the interior leather upholstery and chrome work remained in good condition. In the peeling paint on the door of one, the logo of the US Consulate had been scraped from the door but was still recognizable. Jeep Wagoneers used to be the luxury four-wheel drive transportation of our government. This was the parts storage. But no one drove the Wagoneers anymore.

The Jeeps and the vehicles in the shop all seemed to represent the farmer's ethic of complete self-sufficiency. But it was all out of date. There were no indications of recent activity. Waiting for John Hardbattle to return, I kicked tires of old Jeeps and paced in the driveway as the sky turned darker and gloomier.

Hardbattle finally arrived home at five-thirty. His day had apparently not gone well. His face appeared strained and weary when he got out of the truck accompanied by another man.

"This is Willie." Hardbattle tersely introduced us to the small man beside him wearing a broad-brimmed cavalry hat.

Hardbattle sat down in a chair immediately. His jaw was clamped and he avoided eye contact. I began to imagine disaster. I had no idea what might have gone wrong, or what kind of stress he'd been under, but scenarios popped into my mind. Had he been doing a deal with cattle? Was he angry about his fiancé and child in Norway? Any conversation seemed doomed.

I wasn't sure what we should do, but I hoped things would swing back. The night before, his mood had changed over the course of our conversation; perhaps it would again.

Willie prepared a fire for a *braai*, the term used in southern Africa that refers to the style of cooking meat over an open flame. It occurred to me that food might be the key to bringing a change.

Willie then brought meat from the house, ready for the grill — four slabs of beef, an inch-and-a-half thick.

"Listen," I said, "we want to contribute to this meal. Is there a stove inside? Okay if we go in and prepare something?"

Hardbattle nodded an affirmation.

I nudged Gen and we went to the truck for our food box, and then headed to the house. The box in my arms weighed heavily, and Gen's hands were full. I managed to pry open the screen door with my foot, and then carried my load across the living room toward a dark doorway that I assumed led to the kitchen. There were no lights inside, no electricity.

I lit a candle on the windowsill and we spread an array of produce and other cooking supplies on the counter. The stove was fueled by a tall propane tank. I poured some oil in our cast iron frying pan, put the pan on one of the burners, lit a flame, and the oil quickly began to pop.

"That's too much. Isn't it?" Gen said.

"No, use it all, " I said. I was hoping that food would rescue us from disaster. "Let's cook as much as the pan will hold."

She sliced and diced vegetables and I stirred them in the pan with a spatula. Twenty minutes after we began, I carried a mountainous potato stew into the yard. Willie tended the fire and turned the meat over on the grill.

So far, so good, I thought.

Gen served, filling Hardbattle's plate with a mound of food. At the sight of the full plate his face was transformed and the tension eased visibly. Willie brought out cans of beer from a cold chest and we all sat in a half-circle before the fire pit. On each lap there was an enameled plate heaped high with food.

For several minutes no one spoke. The only sounds were those made by the wind rustling in the trees, mourning doves kuu-ku-ing around us, and metal utensils scraping across our plates. Finally, conversation began with small talk, comments on the food and the weather.

At one point, after a long silence, I asked Hardbattle about Freddy. "You've known him how long?"

"Forty years, I'd guess." Hardbattle pushed food onto his fork with his steak knife. "Our fathers were good friends. James Morris and my father were of the same generation." Hardbattle sawed a piece of meat and took a bite.

"Quite a difference in your ages." I stabbed a peppery chunk of potato.

"Freddy, of course, is much older than I. He was born when his father was young. My father was quite old when I arrived." Hardbattle washed down a bite of food with a sip of beer.

Willie was attentive to everyone's needs. Without saying a word he brought out more beer from the ice chest and placed a can near each of our chairs.

"Freddy has an extremely keen mind for a man his age," I said.

Hardbattle didn't answer immediately. Food demanded his attention and there was a long pause.

"He's led a good life. Freddy is a man who had the power, you know. He was a healer."

"Healer? You mean a shaman?"

He nodded. "A white man entering Nharo culture, you know, and he became one of the most potent healers."

I hadn't known that.

"Freddy was well known as a shaman." Hardbattle opened a can of beer with a crack. "The power sapped him after a while and he had to stop."

"He became ill, you mean?" I was thinking about the herbal remedies that Freddy told me about. I didn't quite understand what Hardbattle meant by "power."

"In some of the cures, the shaman enters a state of half-death. That's what the Nharo call it. It works negatively after a while, and even though Freddy was a great healer, he couldn't heal himself. The power began to destroy his body and he was advised to give up healing. The thing is, it eats away at you — I mean that literally. A healer takes on the disease of the person he's trying to cure."

His tone was animated. There were pauses while his attention shifted to the food on his plate, but he was clearly interested in the topic.

"Freddy still talks a lot about herbal cures," I said.

"Yes, he stopped the ritual healing, but even after that, his knowledge of plants and medicinal herbs continues to be vast."

Hardbattle told me things that Freddy had either forgotten or did not want to talk about. I had seen in Freddy an elderly man who had become smaller over the years, his checkered wool jacket hanging loosely, his hat resting on his ears. But with Hardbattle's telling I could imagine a younger, more vital version of the man — broad shouldered, powerful, and clear eyed — a fearless hunter who could look a lion in the face, or with his head in a leopard's mouth and a twenty-two rifle in his hand, able to retain clarity of purpose.

I knew Freddy had strength and courage in his younger years, but now I learned that he also had the power of a healer and a shaman. *He took on different roles among the Nharo — he was a transforming figure — was he like the jackal or the mantis?*

At dusk the light began playing tricks. We should have been seeing a sunset, but a layer of clouds had made the western sky completely black. At the same time, the conversation had taken a turn I hadn't expected. "You seem to know something about healing and cures yourself," I said.

"I've tried to acquire what knowledge I can over the years. When I returned from England, I felt cut off. Adrift, without a home. Internally, I mean." In the shadows, I couldn't see the features of Hardbattle's face as we talked. I could see his eyes, but no expression. "I inherited this place and it puzzled me that I felt the way I did. I learned about a master, an elder living near Ghanzi, and for several years I worked with him. I was running my ranch and managing the land at the same time. But I wanted a connection to my roots."

"Your Nharo roots," I said.

"Correct. I've been on a pendulum at times. I've gone back and forth. I've lived in separate worlds. Scottish and European culture. Nharo and African hunter's culture. Those two worlds exist in me. I was born into one and raised in another. In one world I lived a life connected to the earth. In the other, I learned European technology and, eventually, how to get rich and stay rich. But what I had in childhood was lost later in life. So, when I realized that . . . that's when I went to study with a teacher. On days I wasn't busy with my ranch, I stayed with my teacher to study medicine. Not medicine in the Western sense, but the mysteries of healing. Bushman culture."

Willie used a thick branch to roll a log over in the fire. For a moment, the flame rose up.

In the light of the flames, Hardbattle's face had an intense expression, but the tension I'd seen earlier had vanished. He seemed to be savoring the food and the company. His level of self-disclosure surprised me. In fact, I found it amazing. In the Garden Bar, he'd gone to pains setting strict limits on our interview. As a result, I'd anticipated that he would limit our conversation to factual background information and insights into Ghanzi history. When he said he'd learned "how to get rich and stay rich," he wasn't boasting. It sounded like an admission of a personal limitation.

He continued. "I learned about the power that arises from ceremonies — the trance dance, especially — and it changed my life. What do you do with knowledge of that kind? Once you begin to learn about it, there's really no turning back. But there I was, leading a crazy life. Running my ranch, living the life of a successful businessman, and on my time away, digging deeper into the mysteries and power of ritual."

He sat forward in his chair, paused, and took a deep breath. "My life changed and things began to unfold. But nothing happened in the way I expected.

"I had an education, and ironically, that was part of my problem, because it became obvious I could never really do what I wanted to do. I could never go back to what I had in childhood. It was an unrealistic expectation, and I began to see that. Studying with the master was fulfilling, but I couldn't take full advantage of what he had to teach. So, after a period of some turmoil, I did the next best thing. I decided to use my skills and the influence of my status to serve the cause of the Nharo and the Bushmen. In making that decision, of course, there was a loss. I had to give up some of my aspirations."

"Aspirations of going back to your Nharo roots, you mean?"

"Well, that, yes. Some inner changes, as well. Things that are difficult to put into words, but that I aspired to all the same. For one thing, the power gained — spiritual power — seems to give a person an inner security. I see that in older people."

"I think I know what you mean," I said. I remembered the calmness I felt sitting in Freddy's yard.

He nodded and went on. "People who have that often seem unaffected by the things that bother me. But I had to let go of my idea of becoming a ritual healer. The more one struggles to hold on to something, the more tenuous the connection becomes. Gradually, you find you hold on to nothing. I didn't want to be left with nothing."

He ate the last few bites of the food remaining on his plate. There was a pause in our conversation. Then he said, "But I'm still on a pendulum. The difference is, I'm headed the other way. The swing of the pendulum is carrying me into my other role. And that's what I will continue with. It's better now that I know which direction I'm going."

Hardbattle's face was silhouetted in the glow of the fire. We'd finished our dinner, though our plates were still on our laps. From somewhere in the distance I heard the whine of an engine. Then I heard the thrum of tires on the cattle guard. The engine noise grew louder. Finally, headlights flashed, silhouetting the arbor and our parked truck. With a roar — pistons hammering, tires pounding on gravel — the vehicle passed through the drive and continued on, until gradually the sound faded to a distant drone.

"One of your trucks?" I asked.

"No. A neighbor passing through. There are several cattle posts to the south. Masire has a cattle post just south of here. He stops in occasionally for a visit en route."

Masire? Did I know a Masire? Then it dawned on me. How could I be so dense? "Masire?" I asked. "Do you mean the President of Botswana? That Masire?"

159

"Yes. He's a friendly chap." Hardbattle's voice was matter-of-fact. "Pleasant fellow. Very outgoing."

I was astounded. Hardbattle was on friendly terms with the President? And still the government deported his fiancé?

Hardbattle seemed to read my thoughts. He set his plate on a log and reached into a nearby thorn tree. Plucking a long pointed thorn, he prepared to pick his teeth. "I know most of the men in the government. Work with them all the time. I like them socially. At the same time, they run a very complex enterprise." He shifted awkwardly and his foot jostled the utensils and plate on the log in front of him. Hardbattle's voice seemed to go flat, as if he was reading from a prepared text. "In the course of their work they make difficult decisions. They'll rub some people the wrong way at times. I'm sure it's nothing personal."

The fire created an island of light at the center of a dark world, and within its shifting reflections we inhabited a dreamlike space. The dancing light animated our faces even when we were sitting still and silent. Willie stirred the logs and the firelight made our small world brighter for a minute. Sparks flew into the air, floated briefly, and resettled into the flame.

Hardbattle rose and entered his house. When he returned, he produced a ceramic bowl filled with brown nuts. He passed the bowl to Gen, who took a couple of nuts and handed the bowl on to me. I took two; they were shiny. I held them in my palm. They were like chestnuts, but a little smaller.

"What are these?" I asked.

"Morama," Hardbattle said.

I stripped the brown shell away from one and tasted it. "Umm. Needs to be roasted. Add salt. It's a little like a macadamia nut."

Hardbattle smiled. "The staple food in the Ghanzi area. Bushmen are thought of as hunters, but they have lived primarily on a vegetarian diet. In every area where the Bushmen live, there is a staple vegetable food. In the Northern Kalahari and in Namibia, the mongongo tree. In the Ghanzi area and south, the morama nut. It has a Latin name, *Bauhinia esculenta*. The nut grows on a vine and forms a huge tuberous root with a root system covering thirty meters. The root is a source of water and the nut contains high nutrition. More protein, in fact, than soya beans.

"Even though the vine grows wild in the veld, it does require some attention, some farming. Grasses interfere with the vine if they get too thick and Bushmen burn the grass periodically to rejuvenate the soil and encourage better growth. Of course, cattlemen object to the destruction of grassland. Wildlife biologists argue that it's an illegal form of hunting. They don't understand the purpose. They think Bushmen are trying to drive herds of wildlife into some kind of ambush. It's not that at all. But the Bushmen are connected to their environment in a way that ranchers and scientists never understand. For Bushmen, their entire life revolves around their connection to their environment. It has survival value, but it also has spiritual meaning.

"Indigenous people all have ways of connecting. It sets them apart from people who live what you might call 'civilized' life. I believe it's true everywhere on earth. Every year, or whenever I can, I attend a global exchange . . . a meeting of indigenous people. The meetings are in Denmark or London . . . some place in Europe. They allow me to hear speakers and talk to a great many people. Indigenous people can share things common to all cultures. Connection with the environment is one common element. I believe the civilized world owes them a debt."

Hardbattle had said that before when he described the way Nharo helped Afrikaners find food in the veld.

He asked, "Do you know about the Sami?"

I didn't.

"They are the indigenous people in Scandinavia. In the far north. You may have heard them called Lapplanders."

"Sure, I've heard of the Lapps."

"Sami is the correct name. They herd reindeer. There's a lot of snow in that part of the world and the people live in houses that have a hole in the roof. They climb through the roof and down a ladder to enter. I saw a model of a Sami house at a conference in Scandinavia. Among the Sami, the shaman practices rituals and makes interpretations about the need of the people. Spiritual or health needs. It's another form of healing practice. The shaman visits each family in his community and makes a gift to everyone. Spiritual gift, you know, not anything material."

"And, that is like the shaman among the Bushmen?" I asked.

"It is, in the healing and the ritual. But the ceremony may begin to sound familiar with the reindeer, the shaman coming from the roof down into the house, making a gift . . . .."

"Our Christmas, you mean," I said.

"Sure. Santa Claus coming down the chimney. Did you know that comes from a ceremony in an indigenous culture?"

"I thought it was northern European — Germanic."

"In the United States, you owe a lot to indigenous people. Your constitution was influenced by the organization of the Iroquois Nation, the Seven States of the Iroquois. The Iroquois were highly regarded by the founders of your nation."

Hardbattle was reminding me of something I'd read long ago in a class — something I'd forgotten.

He continued, "In the civilized world, people generally think they own power. Some people think they can horde it like money. Or they think power flows out of their ego. But power comes from your connection to the world around you."

Hardbattle paused to let the words sink in. "In a hunting culture, a kill is an important event. When a hunter kills a wild animal, he takes in some of the powers of the spirit. A kill in the wild — I'm not talking about 'safari farms' where animals are fenced — but in the wild, it's a transfer of power. Life is based on power. You don't have to think about it in the United States. But, here, everyone thinks about power.

"The images you saw at the Tsodilo Hills. Those are images of power. An artist — in truth, no one in any Bushman culture is an artist because everyone is — a man in a trance state made many of those images. Not just one man — and maybe some were produced by women — over a span of thousands of years.

"Bushmen have been dispossessed. Land has been taken from them. They've lost a way of life. In the process, they've lost power. Lack of power is a cause of disease. It's true for the Nharo, and also for other Bushmen."

"How does that cause disease?" I asked. "Dispossession — I can understand it's a problem — but disease?"

"Disease for the Nharo is a spiritual issue," he said. "In western psychology it would be called low-esteem. The Nharo have a word for it, *kamka kwe*. Meaning the people are weak, inconsequential. They have no power. Disease is a spiritual issue for Bushmen. For Europeans, disease is a result of organisms harming your body. So you have measles, small pox, TB. The Tswana have another idea of disease. For them, disease is the result of witchcraft or sorcery."

"How does herbal medicine fit in to this?" I asked. "Freddy talked about the use of plants for cures."

"Plants are used as remedies for conditions. Herbs are useful if you have a headache, stomachache, or an open wound, things like that. If you get a blister or burn yourself, you don't say you're ill. It's important to remember, medicine is not exact anywhere on earth. Bushmen who live around whites or Tswana get their diseases. Nharo need treatment for TB. Living close to cattle and livestock they get measles, or flu. They also get bewitched and need to see the witch doctor."

I said, "There must be cures for the spiritual diseases the Bushmen suffer."

"Yes, the trance dance, for instance," Hardbattle said.

I remembered my conversation with Hunter in the store at Dkar. He had described the trance dance ritual and how it was being revived and taught by elders.

"A healer has to know about the power of trance," Hardbattle said. "It's a powerful ceremony. The healer, through trance, pulls the disease out. With the help of the community, he identifies and prevents illness through trance. Some of the healers tell you they produce a substance in their stomach that is secreted through their perspiration. It has medicinal qualities. Whether or not that's the way it works, the result is the same. It's a very powerful ceremony, the trance dance. Older Nharo will tell you it's not really a Nharo ceremony. Our ceremony used to be a dance with an emphasis on participation and community. Inducing trance, using the dance to heal, this has been borrowed from the Dzu Twasi, to the north, the people who used to be known as the Kung.

"Dance has always been part of the Bushman's relationship with nature. Anyone can survive in the bush, but people need a way of connecting themselves to nature. Dance produces powerful interpretations from the shaman."

His use of the word "interpretations" puzzled me for a minute. Then I thought that in the healing ceremony there's a certain kind of drama. The drama leads people to an understanding. The understanding, that's the interpretation.

"It's ironic that the increase of disease has brought many people back to their roots. Bushmen have been dispersed. Working for farmers, dislocated to settlements, they've come in contact with members of other groups. More people have felt the need for their own traditional doctors and healing rituals in recent years. So, the cultural practice of the trance dance has been strengthened and it's become more uniform between different groups. If there is a healer in the area and a trance dance is to be held, anyone is invited. You have Nharo and maybe Bushmen from six other groups participating at the same dance in Ghanzi just because they all happen to live here.

"With the dispossession of traditional lands, rituals fell away and became meaningless. Life for most Bushmen became terrifying. So people are rediscovering the value and purpose of their rituals. When you participate in ritual ceremonies, you have to tell yourself, 'It's okay. Do it. Dance. Clap your hands. Join the chant. All will be well.' That's all we have, ultimately. When you find yourself on the brink, looking over the edge, you can always say, 'Let's have a trance dance.' Otherwise, there's nothing."

Hardbattle's tone of voice shifted.

"Once Bushmen are moved to settlements, they cannot carry on their traditional food gathering, to say nothing of hunting. They are forced to rely on handouts."

"Settlements?" I asked. "Tell me about settlements. You mentioned settlements when we talked at the bar in Ghanzi, and I've heard the word before, but I'm not sure I know what it really means. When you talk of settlements, do you mean villages, like Dkar?"

"No, settlements are something else. Fenced areas, 400 square kilometers. Dkar is a village. Settlements are different. Two examples are West Hanahai or East Hanahai, although there are a dozen of them established by the government. Generally, conditions there have to be seen to be believed.

"The idea of the settlements came up after independence. After 1967 and the beginning of a profitable market for beef, farmers just wanted to get rich. They didn't want to put up with groups of what they considered to be squatters on 'their land.' The use of the land was viewed economically after that. If bands of Bushmen were camped on the land, they took up space and that limited the number of cattle and reduced profits.

"In the settlements, the emphasis is on infrastructure. There is nothing of the culture and it's difficult for people to perform the rituals. In all the settlements you will see a clinic, a school, teacher housing, and a borehole. There isn't much else. The settlement idea has mostly resulted in development and better living conditions for the people who come to work in the clinics or teach in the schools. They get to live in a nice government house with running water.

"On the other hand, the Bushmen, the people of the settlement, live in huts, where they often must travel two kilometers to a water tap and the tap is shared with 500 others. They send their children to a school where the teacher has no understanding or appreciation of their culture. The children are treated as if they are ignorant. There is nothing there for the parents, no economic development at all. At the settlements there is nothing of the culture and it's difficult to perform the ceremonies they need."

Hardbattle had been slouched in his chair. "Before you leave Ghanzi, you might get a chance to visit one." Now he sat up. "I think I can arrange for you to visit a settlement so you can see for yourself." As he spoke, John suddenly seemed more comfortable than I'd seen him. Then he leaned back again and looked thoughtfully in my direction. His shift in posture gave me time to wonder what I was getting myself into.

"They don't allow visitors to the settlements," he said. "It's illegal. But it would be important for you to see. You shouldn't take my word. You need to see for yourself."

We stayed at Jackalspits for two nights and both nights it rained hard. On our last morning, Hardbattle was in a jovial mood. The rain had stopped and the air was fresh. Gen and I wiped the water off the chairs and table while he got someone to make tea.

When the teapot arrived at the patio, it was accompanied by a plate of scones. Gen broke off a corner of a scone and tasted it. "Yum, everything's perfect."

"I'd been curious about the name of Hardbattle's ranch, Jackalspits. When I first heard the name it sounded slightly rude, a name adopted for the ranch in a spirit of independence from community values," I said to John.

"A natural water hole," he said, motioning behind his chair in a vague direction. "That's what gave the place its name. Water hole, in Afrikaans, is a *spit*. The watering place was used by a lot of wild animals and maybe someone saw a jackal there once. I don't know about that."

We'd finished our tea and Gen fished for her knitting in her woven bag. I told Hardbattle about the jackals we'd seen in Nxai Pan. "They could easily have disappeared. But instead of hiding, they stopped and watched. Both animals seemed curious. And one started to act like a domestic dog. He shook himself and ran in a circle the way a dog will to start a chasing game. Have you ever seen anything like that?"

John became animated. He laughed and began telling us about hunting and hunting dogs. "Good hunting dogs," he said, "will fan out in order to cover a radius out ahead of the hunter. When a game animal is flushed out, the dogs work as a team. One time I came upon my best hunting dog nose-to-nose with a jackal. The jackal was wagging its tail, its ears perked up, acting like a dog, not a wild animal. He was greeting the dog without aggression. In other words, the jackal was imitating observed behavior. It confused the hunting dog. He smelled a wild animal, but saw the behavior of a dog, like himself.

"Hunting dogs are actually pretty smart, but jackals must be the most intelligent animals around," Hardbattle said. He paused for a second and I expected to hear more about his hunting dog. Instead, his tone of voice shifted in a subtle way. "There is really only one animal that can fool the jackal . . . that can get the best of him."

I waited to hear what it was.

"And that is the cock, the male chicken."

I gave a nervous laugh. By that time, I knew I was being led into something.

"One day the cock was standing in the *kraal* (coral). He stood on one leg the way you see them do when they're resting. One foot tucked under its wing. Just then, Mr. Jackal entered the kraal and saw the cock on one leg. 'Good morning, Mr. Cock. My you look like you're in a bad way this morning. What happened to your leg?'

"The cock looked up. 'I sent it off to the doctor,' he said. 'You know, it was terribly sore and I'm just too busy. I didn't have time to go there myself. He'll send it back in a few days.'

"The jackal's ears perked up. He became very interested. 'I have a splinter in my paw. Do you think you could help me to do the same?' 'Certainly, Mr. Jackal, come over here to the chopping block and we can take care of you . . ..'"

I laughed some more as it registered that the jackal lives his life by trickery, but the trickster doesn't always win. It's a fifty-fifty proposition whether he comes out on top.

When we were ready to leave, we said our goodbyes and Hardbattle waved.

His last words to me had been directions for meeting a man who would take me on a visit to a settlement. I backed the truck out, turned around, and we returned to Ghanzi.

20 Hanahai — The Settlement

Rain was so local, so specific to a single place, it made me think a trickster had taken over control of the weather. Despite the hard, night rain at Jackalspits, the road to Ghanzi was the same pulverized dry dust we had driven on two days earlier.

However, as we arrived in town, we knew the rains were coming, and instead of pitching a tent behind the hotel, we drove to a place in town where we knew we could stay. One of our Peace Corps friends lived in Ghanzi, a schoolteacher named Valerie, whom I'd met when I was on the training staff for her group when they first arrived in Botswana. She generously let us use the spare bedroom in her house. The house had a metal roof and all night I listened to the pounding noise of the heavy rain.

My rendezvous with the man who would take me to a settlement was arranged for early in the morning, and at six I crawled quietly out from under the mosquito net because I thought Gen was asleep.

She rolled over and said, "See you at dinnertime." She and Valerie were making plans to invite friends over that evening.

Leaving the house, I slogged through red mud, wading through deep puddles in places, and followed Hardbattle's directions. The rain was still falling in sheets and the streets were flooded. After two years without rainfall, Ghanzi had become a lake. I walked and waded about ten minutes before I found a tile-roofed, brick building that looked like a former elementary school. My clothing was drenched and my trousers were splattered with red mud from the knee down.

Inside, I had no difficulty finding my guide for the day. He and I were the only men with white skin in the building. Nils was a man of about thirty-five years of age with a round face that was puffy from lack of sleep. He worked for an NGO and was there to pick up supplies. He spoke English with a thick Danish accent.

"*Ja*, good to have company," Nils said. "Such beautiful weather today. I like to have someone to enjoy it with." He attempted a smile, but his mouth formed a grimace and he couldn't seem to make eye contact. Maybe it was too damned early for him to look into the face of another human being.

We were in a warehouse where bags of grain were stacked high on pallets. We stood between piles of cornmeal and sorghum in what used to be a school assembly hall. He clutched a handful of papers and turned his back. "Just let me get organized and we'll be on our way."

Some mornings are like that, I thought, and I tried to stay out of his way. I watched Nils muddle through the warehouse. He wore an athletic-style jacket with leather sleeves. On the back, lettering in red, white, and blue spelled out "Baseball All-American."

When he was ready, I helped Nils carry some twenty-five pound bags of cornmeal across the flooded parking lot to his dirty-white bakkie. He threw the bags into the little truck that was already crowded with egg cartons, buckets, and other supplies. Moving a few boxes into the back, he made room for me on the seat, and we climbed in.

"Yesterday, I drove to Groot Laagte," Nils said. Groot Laagte was a village somewhere in the Ghanzi area. I'd heard John Hardbattle mention the name.

"Every Monday I go there," he said after closing his door. "Three hundred kilometers round trip. That took care of sleep for me. I got into bed at three a.m. And every Tuesday I feel this way. Welcome."

Nils turned the key, the engine idled, and the wipers began to beat. I pointed to the sign over the entrance of the building, "Drought Relief," it said. "Do you think that office will go out of business with the rain today?"

While I laughed at my own joke, Nils looked up at the roof inside the cab as if there might be a translation for strange comments made by Americans.

The truck began moving slowly and he said, "So, today we head for Hanahai. You know it?"

"That's the name for a settlement, right?"

"Two settlements, really. West Hanahai and East Hanahai. Fifty kilometers south."

He guided the vehicle through the small lakes covering the lot and when he came to the street, Nils paused. "You know John Hardbattle?"

"Of course. He's the person who told me to meet you here this morning."

Nils shifted into neutral and the truck rolled to a stop. "Nice man," he said, hesitating. "Please, I must ask you. If you ever talk to someone in a government office or write about this, don't put my name in the same sentence with John's." Nils looked at me nodding with an exaggerated motion. "It's too soon for me to return to Copenhagen."

"I'll remember that. I appreciate you taking me along."

With a grinding noise, he threw the transmission into gear and we began driving carefully through the streets of Ghanzi. As the truck rolled slowly in axle-deep mud and water, I asked Nils about his work.

"Horticulture is what I'm trained for, what I studied. It's my profession. In Botswana they let me to do horticulture work, yes. But I have to pay for it. In order to do any horticulture, I must give people advice on houses to build. Also, I'm a poultry expert now. Of course, why not? I grew up in Copenhagen. Anybody from a city knows all about poultry. So, in addition to being a horticulturalist, I am–what's that good American word? — 'pimp.' I'm a pimp for the chickens. In letters home, I tell my mother I'm the biggest pimp in Botswana so she can be proud of her son's success. Of course, she doesn't know what it means. But it's true. I am the poultry pimp. I help roosters meet hens and help them lay lots of eggs. You'll see. We'll have fun."

His face didn't change expression and I didn't know how to take his last comment. Was he expressing bitterness or making a joke? In the short time I'd known him, I'd become certain of one thing — Nils was nervous about having company today.

We drove past the post office where water cascaded down a slope from a fenced yard and formed a pond on the side of the muddy road. Overnight, the puddles had become public swimming pools and even this early in the morning, naked children writhed in the water, swimming and splashing.

Nils reached into the glove compartment and brought out a chocolate bar. He tore off the wrapping and broke off a piece for me. "Just like my mother taught me. A square meal every morning," he said.

"At Groot Laagte, I grow fifty hectares of morama nuts. Nharo have always gathered the nuts in the veld, but never planted them. The nuts are indigenous to the area and the staple food in the people's diet. That's where I was yesterday . . . and last night."

"Is that what you do then as a horticulturalist?" I asked, "Help them with indigenous plants they can grow for food?"

"Yes, what I try to do. Nharo are not farmers," Nils said. "But they are happy to grow plants that will survive without much care."

Outside of town, we headed south. The unpaved road was full of rocks and potholes. As we picked up speed, our tires crashed into mud holes that threw rocks up against the windows and drenched the cab with a red slurry, rendering the windshield opaque. After twelve hours of hard rain, the dust on the highway surface was as slippery as snow.

"On to Hanahai," he said. "I have meetings there and can't be late. I go to meetings and no one else is on time. But I wait and some people show up. Then I am late one day and everyone goes home." He couldn't see the road any better than I, but the accelerator was down to the floor.

Acacias and thorn trees dotted the flat land we drove through. These were lands that formerly provided rich grazing for migrating wildlife, which the Bushmen hunted. Now the land provided grazing for domestic animals. Cattle, goats, and donkeys crowded the road looking miserable in the wet weather. While most of the animals scampered to get out of the way, the donkeys took their time. They occasionally brought us to a complete stop as they sleepwalked to one side or the other. But Nils had appointments and rather than lose precious time, when he saw an opening, he aimed for it. Leaning on the horn he threaded a narrow lane between the stubborn animals and the edge of the road. More than once, the donkeys held their ground. When that happened, Nils muttered an oath in Danish and I braced myself. The truck swerved, my white knuckles gripped the dash, and the side view mirror slapped a drooping donkey ear.

A few miles down the road, we came upon a long row of large dump trucks with trailers. The trucks appeared to be empty except for the drivers who occupied the cabs and kept the motors idling. Perhaps they were waiting to pick up a load of dirt or gravel, but we couldn't tell.

"Highway work around here?" I asked.

"They must be waiting for the rain to stop." Nils' tone of voice made it sound like the punch line of a wry joke.

"I heard that road improvements were about to happen," I said.

"Yes, progress before our eyes. You can bet it's not going to help the Basarwa."

An hour and a half from Ghanzi, we came to a place between low rounded hills that formed a shallow valley, probably the remains of a river from long ago when it flowed out of a huge lake. Nils slowed to make a left turn into East Hanahai.

We passed under a stand of tall acacia trees. The clouds hung low overhead and the canopy of trees created a dark shadow. Nils guided the truck into deeply rutted tracks. Dunes of white sand edged the road and mounded in the center. The wet, deep sand caused the tires to skid around turns, as if we were on ice.

"Ahh, lovely, white sand," Nils crooned sarcastically. "The beach must be just around the corner."

But around the corner, there was no beach, just endless bushveld and more white sand. Sage-green leaves of low-growing, veld-growth scrub brush along with vines, and grasses covered the ground. Fifty yards from the road, I glimpsed a chain-link barrier.

"What's the fence?" I asked.

"A livestock fence. That's a government euphemism." Nils made a face of extreme distaste. "The government built fences around these settlements and the people complained they were being fenced in. The government's reply, 'Oh no. The policy is not to fence people in, but to fence out the livestock that would come in and eat their food.' So, now the government puts up these 'livestock fences' around the settlement to keep out grazing animals."

As we rounded a turn, a row of white cement block buildings came into view. Nils pointed out a clinic, a school, and a headmaster's house.

"These places give work to Tswana, but not Basarwa," he said.

It was exactly what John Hardbattle had told me.

Improvised huts — traditional mud houses common in eastern Botswana — were grouped beyond the white buildings. People huddled in doorways out of the rain.

"Look at them. They need work. The government feeds them, but they don't have to do anything in exchange. They have no . . . you have a word in English . . .," Nils hesitated.

"Self-sufficiency?"

"That's it. All they can do is accept handouts, they are unable to be self-sufficient."

Nils parked in front of a small concrete block building. "I am looking for the person who will translate for us today. I am going to ask if she is here."

Inside the building a circle of women sat on the floor sewing. Nils stooped over to have a brief conversation with one of them. When he straightened up, he said, "I think she's in the nursery."

We walked outside and toward some dark-green shade netting that hung low over the ground and was supported by poles like a circus tent. The netting covered nearly an acre, and provided shade in hot weather to protect plants from the sun beating down directly overhead. Without it, they would shrivel. A sign said, "Nursery."

We walked under the netting to get out of the rain. Underneath the netting vegetables — beets, spinach, and a variety of other greens — grew in small plots. The plants looked healthy considering they were growing in fine white sand.

"How does this fit into your idea of indigenous food?" I asked Nils.

"An extension worker planted all this," he replied. "He comes over here and works with the people. He'll teach them about these plants and together they all work to keep the plants growing. The problem is, these vegetables aren't part of the traditional diet of Basarwa. Because they've lived well on nuts and tubers from the veld, as soon as the extension worker leaves, everybody goes home. No one feels any responsibility towards this garden. I always try to encourage indigenous plants. That's what Basarwa are used to. But tell *that* to the extension workers."

Nils raised his arm to point out a small plantation of eucalyptus trees waving brown branches in the wind.

"Those trees all died," he said. "The government adviser made us plant them two years ago. Eucalyptus were imported from Australia and they didn't survive the drought. They require water and people wouldn't water them. Whenever I have my way, I try to encourage people to plant indigenous trees that have a chance of survival in a dry spell. But anything indigenous is considered backward by government advisers.

"In another place, we planted an entire hectare — roughly two and a half acres — of indigenous trees. They were all doing nicely until a government forestry adviser drove over and actually pulled up the trees by the roots. He scolded the people for planting them. When I saw the man later, I questioned him. 'Those trees are a step backward,' he told me, 'and I want the people to go forward.' He kept saying to me that he wanted the people to go forward. 'It is very important that they go forward.' " Nils paused and then muttered, "Damn technocrats."

It appeared to me that he wanted to say more, but didn't have the English.

The storm seemed to be letting up. The rain slackened to a steady drizzle, but black clouds hung low and a shower still threatened. Under the netting, a group of people worked at potting small plants. Nils led me to the group and introduced me to Margaret.

"She'll be my translator," Nils said.

Margaret was an attractive woman with skin that was darker than most Tswana. I guessed she was from the Kalanga, a tribal minority in eastern Botswana.

Nils said to Margaret, "I have mealies for you in the back." He was referring to the bags of cornmeal in the back of the truck.

"Good, I've got eggs for you." Margaret said. I enjoyed hearing their conversation. They spoke precise English, she with a rich African accent, and he, with his thick Scandinavian accent.

While I listened to their conversation, I watched chickens pecking under the netting. They picked up seeds, chased insects. I smiled, thinking of Nils' comment in town. He was responsible for all this happiness.

"We're meeting at the school," Nils led the way briskly back to the truck. The three of us crowded into the narrow seat and Nils turned the truck around, back toward the settlement on the other side of the road — West Hanahai.

The ride to West Hanahai took twenty minutes. I had a chance to talk to Margaret and learned that she was taking a year off from university studies to do her required national service. She confirmed that she was a member of the Kalanga tribe and came from a village near where I had taught. In fact, we had mutual friends.

When we reached West Hanahai, Nils pointed out a house built of poles. The poles were placed in a circle spaced about an inch apart. A cone of grass thatch provided a roof. He described it as an easy, but drafty form of construction. Inhabitants tried to fill in spaces between poles with mud, but the mud had fallen away. Termites attacked the poles and large areas of the walls were weakened.

"Houses like that fall down in three to five years," Nils said. "And in the cool season they aren't healthy. In my housing project, I try to show them how to build houses out of bricks molded from mud. Mud bricks in round walls with a roof of thatch make a good house that will last twenty years. With repairs, even longer."

Nils pointed to some mud brick houses in the distance that stood unfinished with walls partially erected. None of them had a roof. "Those houses, standing there without roofs, will only last a few months. In the rain, uncovered bricks will crumble."

His voice seemed tinged with hurt. He was beginning to sound like a person who has made a personal sacrifice and winds up feeling unappreciated. Having been around development workers and volunteers, I recognized the attitude.

"I helped people bring materials here," he said, "but it doesn't help them if I do the whole job. I'm trying to encourage them to follow through."

We drove to a white-painted school building where Nils stopped the truck. "Wait here. This is where we are meeting. Let me see if anyone is inside."

Margaret and I stood outside the truck and chatted while Nils disappeared into the building. Within a few minutes I saw his leather-sleeved jacket reappear in the shadow of the doorway. He walked back slowly.

"Not a soul," he said.

We drove on to a compound of three-pole houses and got out of the truck. Nils explained that he'd been trying to encourage the people who lived here to build a house out of mud bricks.

The three of us poked our heads inside the door of one of the houses, where a group of people sat together in a circle. The stick walls had been daubed with mud, but large pieces had flaked off, and it was drafty inside.

The only piece of furniture was a broken metal chair leaning uselessly against a wall. A stack of bricks three-feet-high and three-feet-wide made the space in the single-room hut even more crowded. Ten men and women were sitting on the dirt floor. I heard the clicking sounds of their speech as soon as I stepped into the room.

We three stood in the doorway while a middle-aged man in a frayed brown suit coat spoke to Margaret in Setswana. The man seemed to be having some trouble with the language, but he spoke evenly. A woman, whom I took to be his wife, interjected comments with greater intensity. The two of them explained to Margaret that they were having problems with the mud bricks.

Margaret translated for Nils, "It seems they have been making bricks for two weeks. They even collected mud close to the village and molded those bricks in a box they made out of scrap wood, using two by fours and tin."

As she spoke, Nils pointed to the mold on top of the stack of brick to show the people that he understood.

The man resumed speaking in his quiet voice. Margaret, translating, said, "These bricks fell apart too easily. The bricks were unsatisfactory. And so, the entire family searched further and found another source of mud. However, that mud had to be carried a long way. Clear from the other side." Margaret gestured with her hand, waving to show that it was a great distance. "Too far to carry the mud back to the compound."

"How far?" Nils asked.

Margaret translated the question, and then gave the man's response, "Ten kilometers."

Nils inspected the bricks closely. He rubbed some of the dried mud off the blocks and crumbled it in his fingers. We walked out into the rain to the pile of unusable mud near the hut. He picked up a clod and broke it under his thumb. Looking at Margaret he asked, "Why are there so many roots in this mud?"

Margaret picked up a piece and smeared it across her pink palm. "We should be planting seeds in this. Everything would grow better."

"Humus!" Nils said. "It won't work for clay bricks. Somehow they found black soil." He sounded frustrated and powerless. "I didn't think it was possible. They're making an effort, though. They're trying."

Margaret's voice was sympathetic. "Oh, I know."

We left the compound without solving the problem of transporting mud for the people to use. "Well, they worked on it," Nils said. "Now, what are we going to do?"

Nils knew mud houses were better than pole huts. But they didn't have the tools, the soil was wrong, and there was no cow dung to help the mud adhere. These problems-on-top-of-problems were beyond his control. The San people were living on land that had been rejected by the cattle ranchers, farmers, mineral explorers, and even the government. Both he and the San were faced with an impossible task.

The three of us again crowded into the front seat of the truck and headed back to East Hanahai.

After several minutes of silence, Nils finally looked over at me as he leaned into the steering wheel, "You can see, we bring progress and success to the people."

At East Hanahai, Nils stopped outside a tin-roofed block building to let Margaret out. We unloaded mealies and Margaret brought two bowls of eggs to the truck. Using the egg cartons piled in the back seat, she filled three of the cartons and replaced them in the back.

"I need to think about this," he said to Margaret. "I maybe bring concrete from Ghanzi next week. We gather rocks and make this house with rocks and cement." He seemed to slump across the side of the truck as he spoke. "But if we do that, what do they learn? Everybody will see that, 'You build their house. Why not a house for me?' " He shrugged. Then, climbing into the truck, he shifted into gear.

"Next week," she waved. *"Tsamaya sentlay!"* Go well.

We backtracked along the road in silence. A few minutes later, we came upon a group of eight or nine children. They scurried to one side as we approached. Nils braked and the leader of the band, a boy about ten years of age, ran to the open driver's side window.

"Re ya mo gate y!" We are going to the gate.

"Hop in."

Shrieking excitedly, the children scrambled over the sides of the truck bed. We bounced for three kilometers until we came to the gate and Nils stopped. The children climbed out of the truck bed and we heard their sing-song piping voices, "Thank you, teacher. Good morning!"

At the main road we began the race back to Ghanzi. The road was still treacherous. We dove into potholes and swerved on the slick sandy surface. To the north was a towering bank of heavy, black clouds. In the west, a deep-red sunset made a gash in the sky.

Lightning flashed and streaked across the black sky ahead of us. As we drove through the former hunting lands of the Bushmen, I remembered something I'd heard a long time ago, a phrase that must have come from an anthropology class, "Follow the lightning." The expression had come from the nomadic Bushmen living in the desert. If there was lightning, there would be water, herds of wild animals, and life.

The noise of the truck prevented conversation and cast a shroud over my thoughts. I didn't want to say anything. The entire day seemed like an exercise in futility. We'd gone to the settlement, but what had we accomplished? Was anybody's life better for it? John Hardbattle had been correct when he described the settlements, "There is nothing of Bushman culture there." At Hanahai I hadn't seen anything of their culture. Other than a few domed grass *scherms* — huts, pathetically clustered to one side of the school and clinic, there was nothing. Crowding did not permit people to gather their own food. Where would they hold a trance dance?

Nils accelerated down the straight road and pulled toward the middle. There was no traffic and driving in the center gave him room for error on the slick surface in case we were to slide. Suddenly, he swerved just in time to miss a mound of crushed rock several times larger than our truck. Other mounds — truckloads of rock — appeared in a line down the middle of the highway. None of the mounds had been there when we drove this way earlier. Apparently the highway maintenance project had begun. I remembered the line of construction trucks we'd seen. They had delivered crushed rock for the new roadbed, but nobody thought it necessary to post signs. I counted twenty truckloads of rock in the road.

Nils had a grim expression.

"They keep drivers on their toes here, don't they," I said.

He made a wry face. Maneuvering the truck along the slick shoulder of the road, he rolled his eyes and seemed unable to speak. We followed a thin line that ran between the piles of rock and the drop off of several feet into the desert at the side of the road.

His foot still to the floor, Nils aimed us toward the part of the sky where lightning flashed against a wall of black. We followed the lightning all the way back to Ghanzi.

It was nearly seven when I arrived back in town. Our hostess, Valerie, a young woman from Queens, had scheduled dinner for five-thirty. I entered the room to find a party in full progress. Several young Volunteers and couples sat around a table chatting and joking. I suddenly became aware of my clothes, wet and mud splattered. My matted hair was plastered across my forehead.

Gen greeted me with a wide-eyed expression that indicated a mixture of irritation and sympathy. "Where have you been?" she asked. "You alright?" She brought me a glass of juice and I sat down at the table.

My head ached from the vibrations of the truck on the road. I couldn't keep up with the conversation. I asked someone to pass the salad and found tears welling up in my eyes. When asked about Hanahai, I tried to describe the people's housing and my words sounded angrier than I intended. My comments all seemed inappropriate, and, in any case, the conversation moved on before the right words came to mind. But finally, I realized I felt grief and just wanted to be alone.

There is nothing that sharpens the focus like being at a party, knowing you're there in body, but your mind, emotions, and spirit are somewhere else. Amid the chatter of friends, people I normally would have enjoyed, I retreated.

I had been witness to a tragedy. It was not the kind of tragedy that a person or family has suffered, but a tragedy for a whole society. I had never observed such a catastrophe before.

John Hardbattle had described the settlements, but the full meaning did not hit me until I saw them. He had told me of people forced to rely on handouts, deprived of the conditions that support a culture and livelihood. Everything I saw confirmed what he'd said. They were people without work or meaningful tasks living in sub-standard housing. When they tried to improve their housing by their own effort, they faced overwhelming obstacles.

These people were not new to poverty. The San had lived in poor conditions for years, as squatters on the dole or laborers under serf-like conditions. At Hanahai, I'd seen the policy of assimilation at work. Children are sent to school to be acculturated, apparently in the hope that the parents' generation, unskilled and illiterate, will die off and be replaced by a generation that will have an easier time blending in. But discarding one generation, causes a social disconnect for the next. What the future holds for them is a huge identity crisis. The probable result is a generation of alcoholism and depression.

I could see the problem — it was the problem of indigenous people everywhere — and I felt helpless.

Hardbattle had told me that for the Nharo, disease was a spiritual issue. He used the Nharo word, *kamka kwe*. I had seen the kamka kwe in East and West Hanahai — the signs of people who felt weak and inconsequential.

His prescription for the problem was the healing. The trance dance.

In my grief and helplessness, I began to realize that I was suffering from the same disease. Kamka kwe.

I began to think about Freddy and remembered that Gen and I would return to Dkar at the end of the week. That dry, dusty village I couldn't wait to leave a week ago, now seemed like paradise compared to Hanahai. It was Tuesday when I met Freddy — exactly a week ago. When I'd first learned about him months earlier, I never would have guessed that meeting Freddy Morris would open doors to experiences like visiting Hanahai.

My mind had made a huge leap when I'd read about Freddy in the newspaper. Acting on the conclusions of that mental leap, I'd driven across the Kalahari. I wondered if I would have followed through had I known what I was in for. But visiting those settlements was an experience I had to have. I hoped I was following the lightning.

21 Return to Dkar

I wasn't able to sleep the last two rainy days we spent in Ghanzi. At night, surreal images replayed endlessly before my eyes. In his wry tone, I heard Nils say, "Ah, lovely white sand . . ." and I saw images of a small dark hut and a crowd of people huddled near the walls. In the rain, I walked under shade netting and looked at carrot tops growing out of white sand. I heard John Hardbattle's voice saying to me, "These are a good source of water." A grove of dead brown trees waved their branches in the wind. I had visions of Nils unwrapping a chocolate bar, and John Hardbattle speaking in a hypnotic drone, "A healer has to know the power of trance."

Over and over during the night, I found myself reliving the experience of racing in a truck on a muddy road toward huge mounds of crushed rock. I saw an image of John Hardbattle in the flickering light of a campfire asking me, "You know about the trance dance?"

In my mind, I saw a San family. I couldn't tell if they were in Hanahai or in the Tsodilo Hills. They were huddled in a small house, and the walls of their hut open to wet, windy weather. At other times they sat in dry sand under a blazing sun and some of them shouted at me, trying to sell me a souvenir.

Then there was Freddy in his yard, scowling, his eyes burning with anger, when he refused to answer my question about the Nharo people.

I saw faces of people I had spoken to in the previous week — young Bushmen, missionaries, development workers, white Afrikaners — all people I recognized, yet my mind couldn't make sense of any of it. Faces rushed past and I kept hearing John Hardbattle telling me, "You need a trance dance — a healing."

At times I awoke as if from a drugged state to hear rain pelting the corrugated metal roof of the house where I was trying to sleep.

Freddy appeared again, a wise paternal figure, who took time to talk to me and my mind calmed as I remembered that tomorrow we were going back to Dkar, and I would see him in two days. We could talk.

I had asked him all the questions I'd thought of to ask, and he had told me everything he could remember or felt comfortable talking about. Now, what interested me was the act that had turned Freddy's life in a direction different from the rest of his community — when he impregnated a young San woman and then refused to keep it a secret.

Freddy's openness had been a violation of a strict code of conduct and it caused a confrontation with his Afrikaner neighbors.

In 1973, Freddy had spoken with Margo and Martin Russell, who were social scientists studying Afrikaners in the Ghanzi area. "I told the whole lot about it . . .. I did not hide it and they were angry, but what does it help to hide it away . . .? Some men were not angry because they did just as I did. They slept with Bushmen . . .. In the beginning nearly everybody was a rondloper." He used the Afrikaans word for "one who walks about" — a hint at promiscuity.

White women disapproved, he said. "They still talked to me, but they held themselves superior. They did not want me to think that I was now going to get a white woman. I did not mind . . . I could not have both black and white, so I hold what I've got."

In his community's view, the Bushmen were a Stone Age people and it was the Afrikaner's duty to keep them in a subservient role. A white man should not even think about marrying a concubine. He should play no role in her children's upbringing. The rules of behavior were a fact of life. Not subject to debate. The rules did not depend on individual acceptance or rejection. The rules were tangible and they imposed their reality upon every member of the society. Freddy's challenge invited ostracism from his community and the wrath of his father.

In some groups, initiation is a formality, a ritual that follows from attainment of a certain age, such as a bar mitzvah. In other groups, it occurs as a result of a test — killing a lion, for instance. But initiation can also happen through events of a life — an experience of loss, such as the death of friends or loved ones. Freddy's initiation was conferred when he made his decision and stood up to both his community and his father.

Life handed Freddy the initiation experience that helped transform a young man into someone who could cross a cultural boundary and later become a shaman and healer.

When Gen and I returned to Dkar, we discovered how localized the rain storm had been. It had never crossed the imaginary line that existed somewhere between Dkar and Ghanzi. Dkar was as dry as ever.

Friday morning, I took my camera and went to see Freddy. I was no longer seeking information or answers to questions; all I really wanted was some inner calm. On my previous visits I'd felt my restlessness diminish during the time I sat with Freddy. When others came into the yard to sit with him, I wondered if he also calmed them. With Freddy, I found acceptance. His temper could be volatile, but when Freddy erupted in response to something in a conversation, he then went back to his normal, unruffled self just as quickly.

After exchanging greetings, I brought out my camera and he smiled toothlessly while I snapped a few photographs. We made small talk about the drought, the quality of mealies in a year when they can't grow their own, and Freddy told me about antidotes for snakebites. Children arrived in the yard for tea and played around us, moving as close as they could to overhear what we were talking about, listening to us speaking in English.

We didn't talk long before Freddy became agitated. He rustled in his chair, cleared his throat, and forgot where we were in our conversation. It was obvious his attention was elsewhere. During a pause, I heard a sound in the back of his throat, "Mmph." He then said, "I must go see my son. There is some talks that we got, over there."

"You need to go now?" I said. "Let's walk over together."

I was wearing open-toed leather sandals and as we walked I kept getting thorns in my toes. Freddy laughed at me when I stopped to pick the thorns out. We walked past the schoolyard where women were shoveling concrete into forms to make bricks. Behind the chain-link fence, children stood in a neat line, metal cups dangling from their hands. A cook ladled hot tea and dispensed thick slices of bread.

"Tea time," Freddy pointed. He might have been suggesting with his gesture that I take a photograph. I knew that he liked being around children.

We walked past the store building painted with zebra stripes and I said, "It's getting warm. Hot already this morning." I was making conversation to fill a silence. "It'll be too hot today."

"Aii! We are like Hawaii." Freddy cackled over his joke. "Where do you stay?" he asked.

I pointed out the hostel buildings where the varnished logs reflected the sunlight. The hostel was two hundred feet away and Freddy couldn't see as well as he used to. I wondered whether he could see where I pointed.

I walked carefully to avoid thorns and saw the dust we were stirring up.

I was curious about something. "The name of Dkar . . . what language is it?" I asked.

"I don't know what language. Maybe Dutch. De a Kar. Dutch. Gowha is Nharo name for the place."

"De a Kar, hmm," I said. "What does that mean?"

"Mean?" The trembling of Freddy's voice gave me a clue something was wrong. I looked at him and saw the familiar glow of intensity in his eyes. I took it to mean that I had just asked about the stupidest question he could imagine. In his impatience, he roared, "Mean? Just the name, Dkar. Gowha. De a Kar. Name of the place."

His roar was like a lion's. It felt satisfying to feel his intensity again.

We were silent for a moment and, leaving the road, turned onto a trail that led through low shrubs.

"Are you going to the workshop then, Freddy?" The building was a hundred yards ahead.

"Yes, I going to workshop."

I was aware of my deference to Freddy. Like a schoolboy, I found myself asking for approval in indirect ways. I didn't want to admit that we were about to say goodbye. I was aware of something in my voice that sounded like a not-quite adult acquaintance. Making conversation to avoid the inevitable farewell.

"Hope the aspirin works?" I said, mixing my statement into a question.

At that moment a group of four people rounded a turn on the path — two men, two women — all of them white. The women wore flower-print sundresses and walked in the front. As they approached, Freddy said, "That would make a nice picture."

I remember his phrase, "The whole world like smoke. Men look like sticks." Apparently, women were still women.

The group stopped to chat. Everyone smiled. They introduced themselves and told me they were missionaries involved in an education workshop in Dkar. They were on their way to Xade, in the Central Kalahari. Two of them were Americans from the Midwest. I told them I was from Seattle.

The couple from the Midwest told me about a bicycle trip they took once to the Pacific Northwest. During the month of May they rode from Seattle to San Francisco.

"I'll bet you got wet," I said. I knew of other bicyclists who had been drenched riding along coastal roads in Washington state.

"We never dreamed it would rain so much at that time of year. It rained every day we were on the coast."

"Quite a contrast between the Pacific Northwest and Dkar," I said.

"Well the average rainfall here is between 300 and 400 mm," the woman replied. "That much," she held her hands out, indicating a distance of about a foot.

"How long will you be here?" one of the men asked.

"Until tomorrow morning. We'll spend another week in the western Kalahari."

As we talked, I become aware that all the remarks were directed to me. Freddy stood quietly nearby and I began to feel uncomfortable that no one acknowledged his presence. I made a point of introducing Freddy. They all nodded, but their manner was cool. No one spoke. A stir of discomfort or embarrassment moved through the group. I took it to mean that they already knew him.

I'd become used to seeing Freddy treated respectfully in his yard by his visitors. When the four waved and moved off, I found it curious that no one in the group had spoken directly to him. So, why hadn't they? I had no idea why, but they had acted with a unified purpose. Following some unspoken, unacknowledged rule that all of them knew about.

Freddy started off in his old man's style of walking, his face fixed in an expression of concentration on every short step. I was still stunned. I had known about the ostracism he'd experienced when he was young. It was a revelation to see how much his past was still his present.

Freddy and I picked our way along the trail between low-growing thorn bushes until we came to the gate of the workshop.

"Is this where you're going?"

"Yes, here. Bye-bye." he said.

I thanked him for spending time with me and waved. Freddy seemed a bit impatient. He shuffled his feet. Rather than prolong the parting, I headed off toward the hostel and, after I'd taken a few steps, I turned to catch one last glimpse of him. I saw the cause of his impatience. His back to me, Freddy faced into the bushes peeing into a clump of thorns.

That would be the last time I would see him.

My final view of Freddy Morris — peeing, his feet planted firmly on the earth. I turned toward the hostel and breathed a prayer:

> *Give me the strength and integrity of a man like him. And one other thing . . . please . . . should I live to be that age . . . I, too, want to be able to pee into the bushes when and where I want.*

22 The Healing

Under the glare of the fluorescent light in the hostel kitchen, a pot of spaghetti simmered on the stove.

Gen added salt and stirred, as I sat nearby keeping her company. As she worked, she talked about how her day had gone.

While I'd been visiting Freddy, she had walked around the grounds near the studio.

"Remember the art teacher?" she asked.

"The South African woman?"

"That's her. Very gentle person. She took me to the art classroom to show me some prints."

"What kind of prints?"

"Black and white compositions. I don't know what process they used. They don't look like block prints, but they're striking. And you have to know the story to really appreciate the art."

"Everything has a story," I said. "The artist's explanations certainly helped last week."

"It's the same with the art work today. Not exactly art for art's sake . . . as far as I can tell, it all has a religious basis. If a person viewing looks for a portrayal of everyday life, they're wasting their time."

"Religious? Really?"

"Not in the Western sense. Religious in terms of what brings people together and makes them feel that they have a community. That they share values and history. In our culture, artists innovate and express their individuality. In the West, an artist might say, "I want to produce art that is like no other." An artist here might question how a person could do art if they don't care about tradition."

Gen interrupted herself to test the pasta.

"Actually," she continued, "I think everyone here is an artist. There is no distinction between artist and . . . whatever the other category is. Community? Artistic intuition belongs to everyone."

She opened a package of powdered mushroom soup and stirred it into the water with the pasta.

"Ah, the Alfredo sauce. The chef's secret."

I got up from my chair and brought plates and utensils to the table.

Gen ignored my comments.

"And the floor was amazing," she said, continuing to stir. Her face wore an expression of concentration.

"The floor? How do you mean?"

"Covered with hard-edged, colorful designs."

She paused again to check if the pasta had softened.

"Apparently, it was a group project, painting the floor. I don't know how it worked. Maybe different artists took different sections. But it turned out beautifully. Like the canvases we saw last week. Everything tells a story."

"Did someone explain the stories?"

"It didn't occur to me to ask. I just appreciated the wild design."

She grasped the handles of the pot with hot pads and pulled it off the stove.

"Time to eat."

After dinner, we sat in the kitchen to read since there was no reading light in the dorm. When the wooden chairs became too hard, we decided to headed back to the dorm. I turned off the light and closed the door.

Gen said, "It would be nice if you'd make tea in the morning."

I agreed.

In the morning I'd even bring it to the room.

The brilliance of a full moon poured through the window as I crawled inside my cone of mosquito netting. The fabric mesh had trapped the hot and oppressive air.

I hadn't slept well since returning to Dkar as my mind continued to be filled with the images of the Hanahai settlement, and as soon as my head hit the pillow, my conversations with John Hardbattle would pop into my head. Any forgotten tidbit would then drive me out of bed to grab my pen and pad and jot it down, adding it to my notes.

This was our last night in Dkar. I had said goodbye to Freddy and my conversations with Hardbattle were complete. Partings bring up strong feelings for me. For days, my mind had been filled with conflicting emotions. The sadness, even grief, reminded me that somewhere in the dark recesses of my mind, I was still grieving for the San in the settlement at Hanahai, but I was tired, and my mind was finally slowing down. As soon as my head hit the pillow this night I fell into a comatose state.

I don't know how long I'd been sleeping when the clamor of voices and rhythmic clapping somewhere across the village awakened me. Moonlight streaming through the window shone directly on my face. I listened for a few minutes and fumbled for my watch. Midnight. The chanting echoed off the walls of the bedroom. For a time I alternated between trying to return to sleep and listening. Staccato clapping accompanied the singing — a group clapping in unison set a steady, quick rhythm, sharply syncopated for a few seconds, and then returning to a slower beat. Several melodies were woven through the singing, women's voices and men's, and then a solo leader above the rest. *It must be a trance dance.* It sounded as if it was close to the hostel. Hunter had told me his people were reviving the tradition.

The sounds reminded me of another night with a full moon as we slept in our tent behind Nata Lodge after returning from the Tsodilo Hills two years ago. I had tried to sleep through a trance dance ceremony that night. I remembered how unsuccessful I'd been. The memories and the thoughts generated by them zipped through my mind. There was no possibility of sleep. This time I wanted to see for myself. Gen was sleeping soundly, undisturbed. There was no reason to wake her. I dressed and followed the voices to find the singing.

The moon, partially hidden behind a wisp of cloud, cast an aura over the flat sandy earth. Acacia thorn trees, drab in the daylight, stood sharply silhouetted against the sky, as did the windmill behind the hostel. A lustrous glow lit the world and simultaneously created vast pools of shadow. The earth looked surreal in the flat, blue light. Dips in the sand became deep wells of blackness. The night was alive.

Rays of moonlight streamed through overhead branches as I stepped across leopard-spotted, snake-skinned sand chased by fears of darkness. Thorns like sharp fingernails seized my shirtsleeves and trouser legs, "Come back! Come back!" I had no choice but to stop to untangle my clothing, and then move on toward the music, and, I assumed, the dancing.

When I reached the firelight, I saw a dozen or so faces, both young and old. I moved close enough that I could smell the burning dung and mopane branches. There were two rings of people around the fire. Men, dressed in animal skin aprons, danced with strings of hundreds of rattles wound around their legs above the ankle. Stitched in stiffened leather an inch or two in circumference, the rattles consisted of dozens of pouches on a string. I'd read that traditionally, those pouches are made from an antelope's scrotum. Inside each pouch were seeds or small pebbles that rattled as a man stamps his feet. The men strutted, shuffled, chanted, and tapped walking sticks rhythmically on the hard-packed sand.

In the outer circle, women, bare above the waist except for their beads, sat cross-legged in the sand, clapping and singing. The steady pulse of their hands maintained a strict rhythm that propelled the dancers with a staccato beat. Step-step-hesitation-shuffle-step.

One of the women got up to join the dancing circle. Then another.

I sat cross-legged in the sand near a shaded bush where my white face would not become a distraction. I was close enough that I felt the heat of the smoking coals.

An ancient woman picked up a handful of twigs and threw them into the pit making the fire blaze up, and the shaman's voice lifted above the rest. As he danced, he swung his arms above his head, waving a whisk made from the black tail of a wildebeest that created a shadow dance in the trees and on the mud wall of a nearby hut.

The shaman's part in the chant was much freer than the rest of the group, as if he were trying to break a chain holding him to the earth. The chanting of the group seemed to lift him. Using different voices, he sang, he called out, he shouted, he talked, and there was a tremor of ecstasy in his voice. Each time, the group responded. Their chanting became louder and wilder. The rhythm picked up in pace. Every call of the shaman was answered by the group. Hands clapped faster; the chanting became more intense. The shaman moaned, his call high-pitched and fervent.

I was hypnotized by the rhythm. Without effort or thought on my part, I swayed and twisted in the firelight. Remembering the mantis who had greeted me on my first day in this village, I moved without bending from the waist up, imagining the way a mantis might move to this music.

Moving with the rhythm, I remembered the day Gen and I went to the art studio and saw the two women outside dancing for inspiration. We had a conversation, both of us wondering about the source of the art. This dance, the complex rhythms, the chanting. I could feel myself giving up control. This had to be the source of that power.

Just then, the leader gyrated and twisted, moaned and stumbled. Reeling dangerously close to the burning embers of the fire, he appeared to fall and then caught himself. The other dancers reached out to him, protecting him from the power that had seized him.

The shaman summoned shadows with his whisk and I began to see an intense light . . . an eerie fluorescent glow. After a moment, I realized it was moonlight. The clouds that had partially covered the moon earlier had passed. The moon was exceptionally large that night, it looked close enough to touch the earth.

I must have dozed, or fallen into a sleep state, because another shape became visible. I was seeing my body in an x-ray view and a second shape danced inside my body. Appearing as a shadow, it danced to its own steps and rhythm. A blurred form, the shadowy edges fuzzy and out of focus.

As the shadow danced, I felt the experience of a shape — a part of myself I had never known. Apparently I was hallucinating. I saw the shadowy figure moving inside my body. The movement seemed to be conjured up by the waving whisk in the shaman's hand.

I closed my eyes and this inside thing invaded my inner recesses, the shape bumping against boundaries built up over a lifetime. The sweep of its motion revealed secrets — private corners inside me blurred, broken, or altered. On overload, I had no way to understand what was happening. What did any of it mean?

I opened my eyes. The dance and the shaman were going at full intensity. It was then that I heard the doves. Mourning doves joined in, kuu-ku-ku. Perched in the surrounding trees, they called in perfect time with the chant. Kuu-ku-ku. Other birds called out; it was strange, songbirds were normally silent in the dark. I remembered the doves two years earlier at Nata, cooing in perfect time with the chanters. Now, it was happening again. In harmony, the singers, dancers, and the birds connected.

At that moment a change happened. Above the other voices, the shaman moaned at every phrase. Shuddering and trembling, he went into his trance. For several minutes his groans continued, before they faded completely. In the firelight and shadow, I looked for him, but couldn't see where he was. Finally, I saw a body slumped on the earth and two women pulling the figure away from the fire pit to safety.

People continued to chant and sing, but their numbers dwindled. Some followed the shaman into trance. Dancers collapsed in the sand. One by one voices dropped out of the chant. What had been a circle, dwindled to only two or three dancers sustaining the ceremony. The singing gradually ebbed completely, falling off into a long period of silence.

For a time, the chanting would start up, continue for a minute, then die off. The shaman lay inert in his trance state and the rest of the group couldn't get the singing started. Around the fire, figures sat slumped or collapsed in the sand. I smelled the musky fragrance of fire mingled with dust and dung and I felt the heaviness in my eyelids. I glanced at my watch. It was three-thirty in the morning.

Somehow, I managed to push myself erect and trudge back to the hostel. Occasionally, I tripped on a low bush invisible in shadow. I was near my room when I heard the shaman's voice groan, trying to revive. He called out a line. A few voices joined in, and then a few more. By the time I entered the room, the chanting was in full swing again. I could hear Gen's rhythmic breathing as I crawled under my mosquito netting.

Chanting and clapping continued until dawn. I was barely awake. A coral pink light reflected off the wall of the hostel room. With the coming of daylight, a dawn chorus of crowing roosters, clucking hens, and braying donkeys joined the chanters. Every dog in the village howled and barked. As the sun rose, the voices and clapping ceased.

I lay in my bed listening and remembered my promise to make tea.

This is the time, said a voice inside. Almost sleepwalking, I got up and trudged to the kitchen, boiled water, and made the tea. When I returned, Gen was still asleep. I set the two cups down on the floor and crawled back into bed. The sunrise felt unbearably bright. Pulling a blanket over my face, I went back to sleep. The kuu ku ku of the mourning doves drifted across the village.

23 Okwa — The Valley of Time

It was midmorning when we left Dkar. The dance from the night before had never really ended; it continued in my mind. I was still living the dance as I drove into Ghanzi late Saturday morning. We had to stock up on groceries and fill the tank. A young man pumped gasoline into the truck while I stood to one side, rhythms of the previous night echoing in my head, gently massaging my brain.

It struck me that we'd be back in Gaborone in a week. Along with this realization, there came a momentary burst of grief. I was saying goodbye to Dkar and Ghanzi. But saying farewell is part of the dance of life. Everything ends in time.

Now, I was going home.

I paid for the fuel and climbed into the cab and we took the road south.

I also felt a kind of satisfaction — I had traveled to meet Freddy and made contact with a San community. During the trance dance the previous night, I'd felt very connected. I'd wanted a direct experience with the San culture and got what I'd come all this way to achieve.

Occasionally, other mental photographs emerged — pictures of the settlement I'd visited. Images of tragedy.

I reminded myself of how I'd felt two years ago. I had been slightly depressed after my visit to the Tsodilo Hills because I had hoped to experience San culture, but considering the language difficulties I'd had, I wondered if it would be possible for me to find San culture and actually experience it. I had no expectations. Then I heard the sounds of a trance dance at Nata. The chanting and hand clapping gave me hope that the San culture still survived in the Kalahari.

So again I was driving through the desert — just as I had two years previously, but this time I had the memory of a night under a full moon with hands clapping, feet stomping, and the chanting of a shaman. The trance dance was tangible evidence of possibility. Leaving Ghanzi, I had a better understanding of the obstacles facing the San. Their culture was still alive, though the world was changing in unpredictable ways. What the future held for the San was anyone's guess.

My mind was racing with thoughts and the minutiae of undigested experiences, but we were then on the same stretch of road I'd driven with Nils to Hanahai. It was, of course, still under construction, so driving demanded my full attention.

The hazards of the road surface pulled me back to reality. The piles of crushed rock that had almost wrecked Nils and me a few days earlier had been graded, the potholes that had thrown opaque mud on our windshield had disappeared, and the roadway had been smoothed over with pink sand and crushed rock. But it was raining and had rained steadily for days. Water had formed pools, and the road surface was saturated, treacherous and slippery as snow.

The mire of the roadway pulled at the tires, threatening to force the truck in a new direction. Numerous times we began a slide, fishtailing unpredictably. Ten miles south of Ghanzi, we slid off the road and careened into deep sand at the shoulder. I turned the hubs on the front wheels to put the truck into four-wheel drive in order to back out.

The roadwork ended before we reached the turnoff into Hanahai. We passed the overhanging trees at the shadowed junction leading to East and West Hanahai. Then, we drove another hour.

By the time I made the right turn into the Okwa Valley, where we planned to camp, the rain had quit entirely. This valley was where a number of expeditions into the Kalahari had begun in the past. The road led us into dense scrub brush where rock protruded from sandy cliffs above.

In the 1950s and '60s, the San in this area lived their traditional hunting-gathering lifestyle, and several teams of anthropologists had made camp here in hopes of contacting Bushmen bands.

It might have been in this place where Elizabeth Marshall Thomas first met the San, those people who seemed so quiet, non-confrontational and shy, who had left their huts and whispered somewhere in the tall grass when the expedition came upon their encampment.

Those days seemed like a once-upon-a-time tale. Holding the wheel, I felt the irony of driving a four-wheel drive vehicle, the same type of machine that has opened up the Kalahari to travel and changed the lives of the San forever. Thanks to improved access in the desert, there was now a rock quarry in the fossil valley. In the distance, I could hear the rumble of highway department trucks carrying away loads of crushed rock and sand.

Our truck rolled and pitched along the road that took us deeper into the valley. Through the dense low-growing shrubbery, we caught one glimpse of a hunter — a man with a bow. It was not a fantasy. I saw the flash of his bare legs and animal skin apron before he disappeared behind a thorn bush.

About noon we stopped along the road to make lunch. I had pulled down the tailgate and slid the food box out, and we were spreading peanut butter on bread when a barefoot San woman appeared before us. She stepped out on the road without a sound, emerging from the brush, walking silently.

She greeted us in Setswana, then hunkered down in the road with her arms hugging her knees, and held that position. The young woman, Gen and I all remained silent for several minutes.

The woman was probably in her mid-twenties. She wore a red blouse of some shiny material and a long wraparound skirt. Her hair was wrapped with a blue kerchief and a string of beads bounced over her chest when she moved. Her blouse and ankle length skirt were much too fine for this thorny, sandy area. I wondered if she was on her way to meet a lover.

I leaned against the truck. The scent of ancient dust mingled with the fragrance of sage. The beauty of the woman's bright eyes and the curve of her breasts under the blouse, made her seem unreal. As I contemplated her presence, I remembered a story I'd read about Freddy meeting a San woman in the desert. I could understand how a man of twenty-four might feel meeting a woman like this in a quiet place.

Gen continued to make our lunch, and she offered the woman an open-faced peanut butter and jam sandwich. The young woman accepted politely, extending her right hand, holding her right elbow with her left hand. The three of us ate without talking, but we could hear the trucks growling near the quarry. When we finished eating, the young woman rolled a cigarette and sat quietly, smoking. After a few minutes, she snubbed it out and rose.

"*Sala sentle.*" Stay well, she said.

"*Tsamaya sentle,*" I replied. Go well. I wanted to wish her luck.

I thought again about Freddy and the young San woman. I had read that they had lain together near a tree and later met on a regular basis. He brought her food; she did his laundry. They made love. At the time, Freddy was tending his father's herd, taking cattle to water. His lover became pregnant and he began to learn about himself. At first he kept it quiet. He knew he'd never be able to take her to his father's house. But word got around. Her family worked for another rancher in the area and others knew her. Everyone talked and everyone knew.

I thought about how, seventy years later, Freddy had a foot in two worlds. Everywhere he went, he carried a dual role. He was two generations removed from many of the residents of Dkar. Freddy was white and that fact separated him from the rest of his family. In appearance, as well as in language, culture, attitudes, they were Nharo. Freddy's status was always open for question because of his white skin. When I visited, Freddy's relatives saw a white man speaking in a strange language with Freddy. Very likely they wondered whether we were discussing things the way white men usually talk, with their controlling powerful words, disparaging Africans.

In many ways, Freddy's view of himself was British. Several times in our conversations, Freddy talked about the Queen, the world of British rule.

Yet there was another way in which Freddy stood in two worlds. He was so old that even though he resided in the world of reality and present life, he already had one foot in the world of ancestors. That gave younger residents a reason to come and talk with him. He'd soon be in a position to intercede on their behalf among the ancestors.

Freddy's words did not always make sense and he was moody — I'd experienced that part of his personality. Undoubtedly, he made requests in the morning he'd forgotten by evening. But while those things might be seen as faults in a younger man, as an elder in the village, they gave evidence that Freddy was crossing into the next world.

Gen and I made camp in the valley bottom, where we had a view of the rounded, brushy slopes on both sides of the valley. The lower hills rose gently like dunes. Others showed limestone outcroppings, eroded and lined with strata. Around camp a flock of guinea fowl clucked foolishly and ran into the brush. Eagles and a goshawk circled overhead.

Okwa Valley made me aware of time in a new way. Time was a force for transformation. Time lent a hand in the process of shape shifting and creation.

Gen reorganized supplies in the back of the truck. I set up our tent. In the spot where I spread tent fabric and pounded stakes, a river had once carried water from a lake. The river had flowed ten thousand — or even twenty thousand — years ago. The place was dry now, though near our camp a slight trickle from a spring brought water to the surface and animals came to drink. As I arranged the tent poles, two small antelope cautiously approached the spring.

There was no longer water flowing through the river valley, only time. At the base of the valley walls with limestone and sand and aged strata, the river of time rushed over me. I felt the flood of past events — the lives of the people who had lived here and the memories of Freddy and his past. I wondered about the future of the San, whose land this was, and who were now a dispossessed people. What would happen to them?

Over the top of the tent, I fitted the rain fly and weighted it down with heavy rocks.

Nothing was determined. Everything, even a river, is subject to change.

Freddy was a man born at a particular moment, into a particular family and milieu. Currents of history pushed against him, as they do for everyone. He yielded to some of those currents, but not all of them. He made choices, rejecting some attitudes and adopting others.

I had choices, as well. I remembered the fears I experienced when my teaching job in Botswana came to an end followed by my periodic upsurges of anxiety. I was afraid of facing life without the security of a job or the regular income I was so used to. And then there was my fear of saying good-bye.

Freddy had survived encounters with both a lion and a leopard. His experiences put my fears into perspective.

The trance dance came back to me. In my mind, I heard the hands clapping, feet stomping, and the chanting with the shaman. My thoughts went back in time and I smiled as I remembered the frightened child of eight or nine who used to come home to an empty house after school. The boy put on a recording from his father's collection, a tribal group that chanted with a shaman in call and response fashion. The boy chanted along with them, facing his fears of being alone.

Our camping chores finished, Gen headed for a comfortable spot under a tree to read and sketch. I took a pair of binoculars and walked up the side of the hill behind our camp. From a rock promontory, I gazed over the valley at the limestone hills. Focusing the binoculars farther north, I could see storm clouds building and was able to make a prediction of the future: We were going to get rained on in the night. It wouldn't be the first time.

Acknowledgments

During the time I was gathering the information for this book, I was welcomed by Freddy Morris and John Hardbattle. In both cases our conversations lasted for several days and I continue to value their openness and generosity.

I offer a thank you to all the people, friends scattered from Seattle to Gaborone, Botswana, who have given me helpful comments and guidance on the manuscript over the years.

The Wednesday Night Writers Critique group has contributed many useful suggestions in helping me shape the text.

My editor, Mary Beth Abel, has been tenacious, wise, and patient, steering me in constructive directions. She has provided immeasurable assistance with the many decisions that have had to be made.

Thanks as well to Marian Haley Beil at Peace Corps Writers for her exceptional effort in the design of the book and editing.

Finally, a thank you to my wife, Genevieve, for participating in an adventure, and for allowing interruptions in her life whenever I asked her to take time to read sections of my manuscript and make suggestions on style or tone. Genevieve put her artistic talent to work, as well. Her mantis design has been a marvelous addition to this book.

Bibliography with Endnotes

Opening quotation

Bleek, W. H. I. *The Mantis and His Friends: Bushman Folklore.* Collected by the Late Dr. W.H.I. Bleek and the Late Dr. Lucy C. Lloyd. Edited by D.F. Bleek. Cape Town, London and Oxford: T. Maskew Miller, Basil Blackwell, 1923.

> Illustrated with many reproductions of Bushman drawings.

Prologue

Lewis-Williams, J. David. *Believing and Seeing: Symbolic Meanings in Southern San Rock Paintings.* London: Academic Press, 1981.

Thomas, Elizabeth Marshall. *The Harmless People.* New York: A.A. Knopf, 1959.

Van Der Post, Laurens. *Lost World Of The Kalahari.* London, Hogarth Press, 1958.

Vinnicombe, Patricia. *People of the Eland: Rock Paintings of the Drakensberg Bushmen as a Reflection of Their Life and Thought.* Pietermaritzburg: University of Natal Press, 1976.

Chapter 1. Losing Our Way in the Kalahari
Chapter 2. A Flip Remark
Chapter 3. A Stroke of Luck

Mason, Tamar. "Profile: Oom Freddy Morris." *Mmegi/The Reporter*, Gaborone, Botswana. March 20–26, 1992.

This article is referred to several times in the book.

Chapter 4. Orwell Meets the San

The conversation in the University of Botswana cafeteria in this chapter is a composite of several conversations and information obtained from the sources listed below.

"Butale Responds To Basarwa Report." *Mokaedi: Monthly Newsletter of the Botswana Christian Council* 1, September 1992.

"Comment." *The Gazette*, Gaborone, Botswana. June 3, 1992.

The main point of this editorial was that the Basarwa "must be heard."

Editorial. "Plight of the San." *The Botswana Guardian*, Gaborone, Botswana. June 19, 1992.

"Ernest Moloi, in Windhoek, Reports on Barsarwa Conference." *The Guardian*, June 19, 1992.

Finley, Bruce. "Water Wars Come to Botswana, Rapid Expansion of Economy Creates Demand for Bushmen's Resources." *San Francisco Chronicle*, San Francisco, California. January 14, 1992.

Gazette Reporter. "We Were Insulted — Basarwa." *The Botswana Gazette*, Gaborone, Botswana. June 3, 1992.

Kelso, Casey. "Hungry Hunter-Gatherers Tortured." *Weekly Mail*, South Africa. July 24–30, 1992.

Kelso, Casey. "The Inconvenient Nomads Deep Inside the Deep." *Weekly Mail*, South Africa. July 24–30, 1992.

Kgaswe, Linchwe. "Botswana Authorities Dismiss Human Rights Allegations." *The Midweek Sun*, Gaborone, Botswana. October 23, 1991.

Leepile, Methaetsile. "Basarwa: The Local Issues." *Mmegi/The Reporter*, Gaborone, Botswana. June 19–25, 1992.

Meyer, Clifford. "RADs and Basarwa Do Not Mean the Same — Legwaila." *Mmegi/The Reporter*, Gaborone, Botswana. October 9–15, 1992.

Mogwe, Duncan. "Policy To Have Positive Implications For Barsarwa." *The Midweek Sun*, Gaborone, Botswana. August 12, 1992.

Moloi, Ernest. "Minority Rights Issue Featured Prominently in the 1992." *The Botswana Guardian*, Gaborone, Botswana. September 25, 1992, Special Supplement ed.

Ramsay, Jeff. "A Lost World That Never Was." *Mmegi/The Reporter*, Gaborone, Botswana. June 12–18, 1992.

Ramsay, Jeff. "Basarwaland." *Mmegi/The Reporter*, Gaborone, Botswana. June 5–11, 1992.

Ramsay, Jeff. "The Harmed People." *Mmegi/The Reporter*, Gaborone, Botswana. June 19–25, 1992.

"Wildlife Atrocities Exposed: Barsawa Speak Out." *Mokaedi: Monthly Newsletter of the Botswana Christian Council* 1(6), Gaborone, Botswana. September 1992.

Chapter 5. The Search

Bleek, D. F. *The Naron, a Bushman Tribe of the Central Kalahari*. Cambridge: University Press, 1928.

Bleek, W. H. I. *The Mantis and His Friends: Bushman Folklore*. Collected by the Late Dr. W.H.I. Bleek and the Late Dr. Lucy C. Lloyd. Edited by D.F. Bleek. Illustrated with Many Reproductions of Bushman Drawings. Cape Town, London and Oxford: T. Maskew Miller, Basil Blackwell, 1923.

> The Bushmen encountered by the Bleeks over a century ago did not worship the Mantis. Dorothea Bleek explained, "They prayed to his creation, the Moon, and other heavenly bodies." The Mantis — the trickster — was a dream Bushman, and the stories found in *The Mantis and His Friends* portray Bushman family life.

Dugard, Martin. *Into Africa: The Epic Adventures of Stanley & Livingstone*. New York: Doubleday, 2003.

Heinz, Hans Joachim., and Marshall Lee. *Namkwa*. London: Cape, 1978.

Jeal, Tim. *Livingstone*. New York: G.P. Putnam's Sons, 1973.

> Livingstone came to Africa in the 1840s as a missionary to make converts in Africa. In his writings, he was always conscious of his audience in London, the potential contributors to his missionary work. He stated his frustrations in Christian terms. But, his true work became exploration and it took him further and further from the mission school. This is in part due to coming to an early understanding about how difficult it would be to convert Africans to Christianity in spite of his rigid personality and fixed ideas. As he became proficient in Setswana, he realized that the standard Christian gospel and lessons, in translation, became absurd. For instance, his listeners took the phrase "God so loved the world . . ." to mean that God's feelings toward Earth were sexual. And when Livingstone spoke of sin, he had further difficulty appealing to his listeners; the best Setswana word he could come up with translated as "cow dung."

Lewis-Williams, J. David., and Thomas A. Dowson. *Images of Power: Understanding Bushman Rock Art*. Johannesburg: Southern Book Publishers, 1989

> This book contains references to W. H. Bleek.

Livingston, David. *Missionary Travels and Researches in South Africa*, New York: Harper & Brothers, 1857. Project Gutenberg EBook, 2006. http://www.gutenberg.org/files/1039/1039-h/1039-h.htm.

Main, Michael. *Kalahari: Life's Variety in Dune and Delta*. Johannesburg: Southern Book Publishers, 1987.

Russell, Margo, and Martin Russell. *Afrikaners of the Kalahari: White Minority in a Black State*. Cambridge: Cambridge University Press, 1979.

> Biographical information about Freddy Morris and his father are on page 90 of this book. Community norms related to sexual liaisons between white men and Bushmen women are also described. The photograph of Freddy Morris and his family is located on page 91.

Silverbauer, George. *Bushman Survey: Report to the Government of Bechuanaland*. Bechuanaland: Bechuanaland Government. February, 1965.

Chapter 6. On the Train
Chapter 7. Circling of Storks
Chapter 8. Into the Desert

The historical references stated in this chapter were shared with me through conversation and interviews conducted in Botswana.

Chapter 9. In the Pans

The quotations of Livingstone's writings in this chapter are from:

> Livingston, David. *Missionary Travels and Researches in South Africa*. New York: Harper & Brothers, 1857.
>
> http://www.gutenberg.org/files/1039/1039-h/1039-h.htm. Project Gutenberg EBook, 2006.

Chapter 10. Mirage

I first came across the Kierkegaard quotation in this chapter in:

> Auster, Paul. *The Invention of Solitude*, New York: Penguin. 1988

The full quotation is found on page 69.

Chapter 11. Meeting the Trickster

The quotations of Livingstone's writings in this chapter are from:

> Livingston, David. *Missionary Travels and Researches in South Africa*. New York: Harper & Brothers, 1857. Project Gutenberg EBook, 2006. http://www.gutenberg.org/files/1039/1039-h/1039-h.htm.

Chapter 12. Into Unknown Territory
Chapter 13. Looking into the Lens
Chapter 14. Hunter
Chapter 15. Suspicion
Chapter 16. The Scar

Chapter 17. Pieces of a Puzzle

De Klerk, Willem Abraham. *The Puritans in Africa: A Story of Afrikanerdom.* London: Rex Collings, 1975.

> The book provides an excellent history of relations between Afrikaners and English. Afrikaners were poor white farmers and socially located between the English and the native Africans. The book covers topics such as how the Afrikaners became "lost in Africa," their psychology of defeat related to depending on Africans and the pressure to look down on them in an attempt to be socially better, and how marriage worked between English and Afrikaans speakers. In particular, the book discusses the conflicting attitudes caused by an upbringing in which white, Afrikaner children, nurtured by African women and raised with African playmates, were taught never to have sexual relations with Africans.

Hunt, William. *Through the Kalahari Desert; a Narrative of a Journey with Gun, Camera, and Note-book to Lake N'Gami and Back.* Cape Town: C. Struik, 1973.

> This book was originally written in 1886. William Hunt published under the pseudonym "Gilarmi A. Farini." Hunt, as Farini, is an extremely unreliable author, a liar in many instances, but also a colorful character. He was an American showman and traveled in the Kalahari, apparently with the purpose of acquiring Bushmen to display in his shows at Coney Island and in his London theater. His many inaccuracies and misstatements of fact are discussed in two books devoted to the subject:
>
> > Clement, A. John. *The Kalahari and Its Lost City.* Cape Town: Longmans, 1967,
> >
> > Goldie, Fay. *Lost City of the Kalahari.* Cape Town: A.A. Balkema, 1963.
>
> However, these scholars believe Farini's writings provide accurate descriptions of the makeup of an ox-drawn wagon and supplies necessary in the desert.

Chapter 18. The Garden
Chapter 19. Jackalspits
Chapter 20. Hanahai—The Settlement
Chapter 21. Return to Dkar

> The quotations in this chapter are from:
>
> > Russell, Margo, and Martin Russell. *Afrikaners of the Kalahari: White Minority in a Black State.* Cambridge: Cambridge University Press, 1979.

Chapter 22. The Healing
Chapter 23. Okwa — The Valley of Time

> I was saddened when I learned of John Hardbattle's death about two-and-a-half years after I met him. Since that time, however, the World Wide Web has made a fair amount of information available about his

life. Wikipedia, for instance, provides a sketchy outline of his life and activities, and most valuable, it provides a bibliography for further reading.

A book that includes a lengthy section dealing with Hardbattle's biography is:

> Gall, Sandy. *The Bushmen of Southern Africa: Slaughter of the Innocent*. London: Chatto & Windus, 2001.
>
> The author is a Scottish journalist.

The work of John Hardbattle's organization, First People of the Kalahari (FPK), was carried on by Roy Sesana until 2013. As with Hardbattle, Sesana's work may be easily researched on the Web.

The main purpose of the FPK was to fight for the land rights of the Bushmen and counter the government's position that nomadic people have no right to own land. Over time this government policy has forced Bushmen into working for wealthy farmers at low wages. The work of FPK was largely supported by income-generating projects such as raising ostrich and poultry.

In the absence of the FPK, there are several international organizations that support the cause of indigenous peoples:

- Cultural Survival (www.culturalsurvival.org)
- First Peoples Worldwide (www.firstpeoples.org)
- International Work Group for Indigenous Affairs (www.iwgia.org).

Though they are not specifically devoted to the Kalahari Bushmen, they do represent the Bushmen cause in influential places like the United Nations and academic circles.

The Kuru Development Trust, now called the Kuru Art Project, was established in 1990 to assist active participation by Bushmen in their economic development and to support Bushmen land rights. (www.kuruart.com)

Made in the USA
Charleston, SC
03 January 2016